tsumiki

Margaret Lee

つみき

積木

1

NELSON
CENGAGE Learning

Australia • Brazil • Japan • Korea • Mexico • Singapore • Spain • United Kingdom • United States

NELSON
CENGAGE Learning™

Tsumiki 1 Student book
1st Edition
Margaret Lee

Text design: Patricia Tsiatsias Heather Jones
Text illustrator: Tomomi Sarafov
Cover design: James Lowe
Cover photo: International Society for Educational
    Information, Inc, Japan
Illustrations: Tomomi Sarafov
Editor: Monica Pinda
Project editors: Jo Tayler
Publishing editor: Col Cunnington
Production controller: Selina Brendish
Manuscript typist: John Lee
Typeset in Australia by Post Pre-Press

Any URLs contained in this publication were checked for
currency during the production process. Note, however,
that the publisher cannot vouch for the ongoing currency
of URLs.

For product information and technology assistance,
in Australia call 1300 790 853;
in New Zealand call 0508 635 766

For permission to use material from this text
or product, please email **aust.permissions@cengage.com**

National Library of Australia Cataloguing-in-Publication Data
Lee, Margaret
    Tsumiki. 1.

    For year 7/8 students.
    ISBN 9780170102674

    1. Japanese language– Textbooks for foreign   speakers-English-Juvenile
literature. 1. Title.

495.68

Cengage Learning Australia
Level 7, 80 Dorcas Street
South Melbourne, Victoria Australia 3205

Cengage Learning New Zealand
Unit 4B Rosedale Office Park
331 Rosedale Road, Albany, North Shore 0632, NZ

For learning solutions, visit **cengage.com.au**

Printed in China by CTPS
6 7 8 9 10 11 12 12 11 10 09 08

Contents

Introduction

Tsumiki means 'building blocks'. This is a course designed to give you a solid foundation of Japanese language on which you can build to suit your particular needs and interests. It recognises that, while students may learn differently, they all need a clear, easy-to-follow structure that builds on existing knowledge. Learners also like challenges that are achievable and useful.

The *Tsumiki Student Book* provides the language elements that you will need to embark on your language-learning adventure. All the language patterns and phrases that it presents are used frequently in daily communication. Options are available within the course to ensure that you are able to express a range of ideas relevant to your own experience.

The course is developed around the experiences of two students, Andrew and Mariana, who have been learning Japanese in preparation for a visit to Japan.

Script

Before Andrew and Mariana leave for Japan in Unit 6, they have to learn the Japanese scripts **hiragana** and **katakana**. They soon realise when they arrive in Japan how lucky they are to have done so. Without an understanding of these scripts, the world around them would be very confusing indeed!

Katakana and hiragana are introduced in Units A and B of *Tsumiki 1*. As all Japanese is written in script, it is important to have a good mastery of at least hiragana before moving on to Unit 1. If you can learn some of the vocabulary that appears with the hiragana characters in Unit B, you will find it useful later on.

Unit 1 Me

Andrew and Mariana have their first Japanese language learning lessons in Australia and New Zealand respectively. They then use their skills to introduce themselves to Japanese visitors to their schools.

Unit 2 Numbers

It's amazing how often we use numbers in conversations. In this unit, Andrew and Mariana engage in further dialogue with their visiting friends. They can now tell their age, give their year level at school and share phone numbers.

Unit 3 Friends

Having Japanese visitors at their schools has given Andrew and Mariana a great opportunity to find out about life in Japan. They talk about the sports, musical instruments and foreign languages that they learn.

Unit 4 School

In this unit, Andrew and Mariana compare their school experience with that of their friends from Japan. They talk about what they study and what their daily routine includes.

Unit 5 Families

Andrew and Mariana have the opportunity to invite their Japanese friends home. They share information about their family members, their occupations and the places where they work. They also talk about their pets.

Unit 6 Bound for Japan

By now, Andrew and Mariana are ready to visit Japan. While on board the aircraft, they use their Japanese language skills with the flight attendants and with other passengers. They are able to order food and talk generally about what they like to eat and drink.

Unit 7 My host family

Andrew and Mariana know that they will learn lots while they are staying with their Japanese host families. They learn that the key to finding out anything is to ask. Their hosts don't mind a lot of questions about what is what—they are flattered that their guests are interested. Living with another family means that it is important for you to understand who can use what. Expressing 'mine' or 'yours' becomes important.

Unit 8　Birthdays

Andrew and Mariana celebrate their birthdays during their stay in Japan. They soon learn how to wish someone a happy birthday and how to express dates.

Unit 9　Daily routines

By this stage, Andrew and Mariana can help a conversation along by making suitable exclamations and comments. They have worked out that telling the time is simple but necessary for life in Japan, and they start describing a range of things that they do.

Unit 10　Youth culture

How young people spend their spare time in Japan is of keen interest to both Andrew and Mariana. There are so many places to see and things to do in Japan before returning home. They learn how to describe a range of activities and they can talk about how to get from one place to another—a skill that is extremely useful when you are in a big city.

Enjoy your studies and make learning a lifelong passion. *Gambatte!* (Stick at it!)

Margaret Lee

How to use this book

This symbol indicates that the material has been recorded on the audio CDs, so that you can listen to native Japanese speakers saying it.

Shaded panels with a 'key' symbol show the core vocabulary introduced on that page. You should try to learn these Japanese words.

<ruby>覚<rt>おぼ</rt></ruby>えましょう

This heading appears above each sentence pattern and means 'Let's memorise this'. It is reminding you that you should try to learn the sentence pattern by heart.

<ruby>書<rt>か</rt></ruby>きましょう

This heading appears above sections where kanji is introduced. It means 'Let's write'.

This kanji, pronounced れい, means 'an example'. It introduces a model to help you do something.

3

This numbered symbol in the margin tells you that there is an activity in the accompanying workbook to help you develop your language skills.

 セルフ テスト

This heading means 'self-test' and introduces review questions at the end of Units 1–10 for you to check your understanding.

 <ruby>日本<rt>に ほん</rt></ruby>について <ruby>日本語<rt>に ほん ご</rt></ruby>について

These headings mean 'About Japan' and 'About Japanese'. The text and photos in these panels will give you information about Japan's fascinating history and rich, vibrant culture.

This symbol indicates extension material that provides you with a challenge.

A カタカナ Katakana

Outcomes

By the end of this unit, you should be able to:

- understand the development of the Japanese language
- read and write katakana both individually and in words.

A Japanese script

All languages are in a constant state of change and development. Until Chinese Buddhist monks came to Japan in about AD 400–500, there was no written Japanese language. However, by the 900s the Japanese were using three scripts, which are all still in use today.

---

1   **Kanji** is the writing script borrowed from Chinese. Most nouns and the important parts of verbs, adjectives and adverbs can be written in kanji. For example:

ni hon
日本   Japan

ni hon go
日本語   Japanese language

ben kyou shi te i ma su
勉強 しています I am studying.

---

2   **Hiragana** is a 46-syllable phonetic system that was developed by simplifying and rounding Chinese kanji. For every Japanese sound, there is an equivalent hiragana or combination of hiragana.

   a   Hiragana can be used instead of kanji, so that children and language learners read and write Japanese sooner.

ni hon go
日本語 (Japanese language) can be written as にほんご.

ben kyou
勉強 (study) can be written as べんきょう.

   b   So that learners of Japanese can read kanji, you often see small hiragana written above the kanji. These small hiragana are called furigana. For example:

べんきょう
勉 強   ← —— Furigana

   c   Hiragana is used for special purposes in Japanese grammar. An example is shown in the highlighted part of this sentence:

ben kyou shi te i ma su
勉強   しています。   ← This is the end of the verb and shows its tense.

---

3   **Katakana** was created by simplifying kanji even more than was the case for hiragana. Every Japanese sound can be written using a single katakana or a combination of katakana.

   a   Katakana is used to write foreign or 'loan' words (that is, words that have come to Japan from other countries). For example:

   ベン   Ben   チョコレート   chocolate

   b   Katakana is also often used in advertisements.

Advertisement for
The Lion King

Katakana—Pronunciation

Katakana is a phonetic script consisting of 46 basic characters plus a straight line.

Each character represents either a vowel or a consonant plus a vowel. There is also a character for the sound 'n'.

Each vowel is pronounced as follows:

ア (a) is pronounced like the **a** in p**a**pa.

イ (i) is pronounced like the **i** in p**i**t.

ウ (u) is pronounced like the **u** in p**u**t.

エ (e) is pronounced like the **e** in p**e**t.

オ (o) is pronounced like the **o** in p**o**t.

The two katakana for 'bus' run from top to bottom on this Miyajima bus-stop sign.

日本語について Traditionally, Japanese is read from right to left and vertically from top to bottom. This is still frequently the case (and this style has been used in the script charts in *Tsumiki*), but it has become more common to write horizontally from left to right.

B2

Clues for learning script

- Study each katakana until you are familiar with it when you are first taught it so that you only have a few to learn at a time.
- Carefully follow the instructions for writing each katakana. Write them out as many times as you need to remember them. Use handouts from your teacher and those in your Workbook to help you.
- Study the picture provided with each katakana. You will remember the katakana more quickly if you visualise each katakana script within a picture. This technique should also help you remember the correct pronunciation.
- Read the sentence next to each picture. The letters in bold italic give you the pronunciation of the katakana.
- While you practise, keep your student text open at the page where each katakana is introduced.

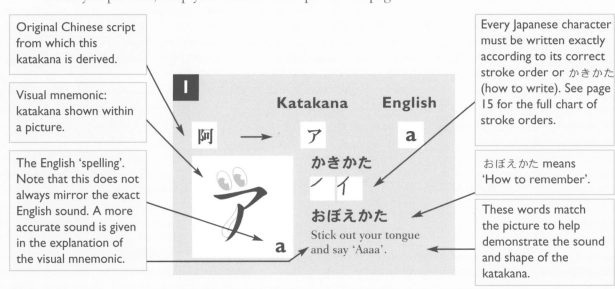

Original Chinese script from which this katakana is derived.

Visual mnemonic: katakana shown within a picture.

The English 'spelling'. Note that this does not always mirror the exact English sound. A more accurate sound is given in the explanation of the visual mnemonic.

Every Japanese character must be written exactly according to its correct stroke order or かきかた (how to write). See page 15 for the full chart of stroke orders.

おぼえかた means 'How to remember'.

These words match the picture to help demonstrate the sound and shape of the katakana.

The first set

In this unit, you will be introduced in stages to each of the basic katakana sounds and many of the combination sounds. The first set of fifteen, as highlighted in the chart below, should be read right to left.

ワ wa	ラ ra	ヤ ya	マ ma	ハ ha	ナ na	タ ta	サ sa	カ ka	ア a
	リ ri		ミ mi	ヒ hi	ニ ni	チ chi	シ shi	キ ki	イ i
	ル ru	ユ yu	ム mu	フ fu	ヌ nu	ツ tsu	ス su	ク ku	ウ u
	レ re		メ me	ヘ he	ネ ne	テ te	セ se	ケ ke	エ e
ン n	ヲ o	ロ ro	ヨ yo	モ mo	ホ ho	ノ no	ト to	ソ so	コ ko	オ o

1

Katakana English

阿 → ア **a**

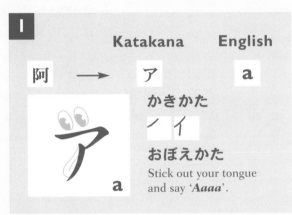

かきかた
ノ ア

おぼえかた
Stick out your tongue
and say '**A**aaa'.

2

Katakana English

伊 → イ **i**

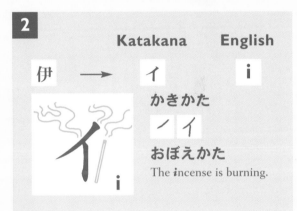

かきかた
ノ イ

おぼえかた
The **i**ncense is burning.

3

Katakana English

宇 → ウ **u**

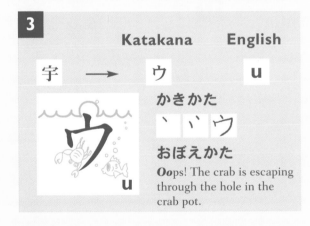

かきかた
丶 ウ ウ

おぼえかた
Oops! The crab is escaping
through the hole in the
crab pot.

4

Katakana English

江 → エ **e**

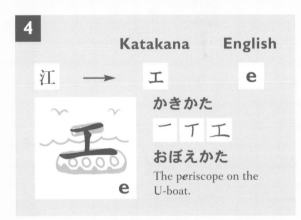

かきかた
一 エ エ

おぼえかた
The p**e**riscope on the
U-boat.

5

Katakana English

於 → オ **o**

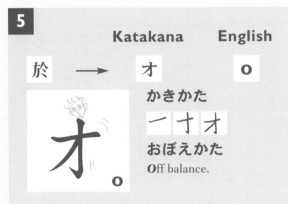

かきかた
一 オ オ

おぼえかた
Off balance.

6

Katakana English

加 → カ **ka**

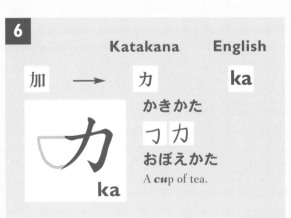

かきかた
コ カ

おぼえかた
A **cu**p of tea.

7

Katakana English

幾 → キ **ki**

かきかた
一 ニ キ

おぼえかた
Kindling for a campfire.

8

Katakana English

久 → ク **ku**

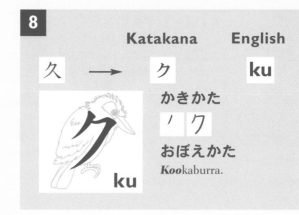

かきかた
ノ ク

おぼえかた
Kookaburra.

9

Katakana English

介 → ケ **ke**

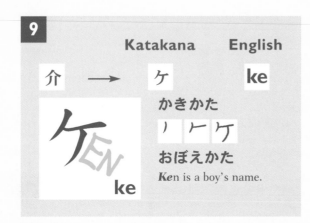

かきかた
ノ ト ケ

おぼえかた
Ken is a boy's name.

10

Katakana English

己 → コ **ko**

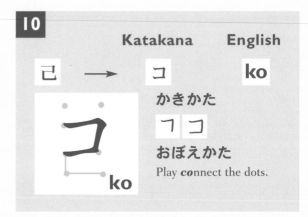

かきかた
フ コ

おぼえかた
Play **co**nnect the dots.

11

Katakana English

散 → サ **sa**

かきかた
一 十 サ

おぼえかた
Very few trees grow in
the **Sa**hara Desert.

12

Katakana English

之 → シ **shi**

かきかた
丶 丶 シ

おぼえかた
A sinking **shi**p.

13

Katakana English

須 → ス **su**

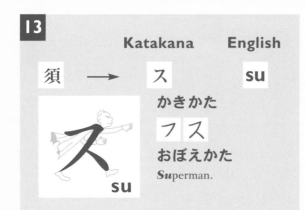

かきかた
フ ス

おぼえかた
Superman.

14

Katakana English

世 → セ **se**

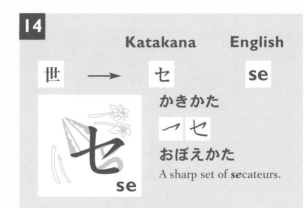

かきかた
一 セ

おぼえかた
A sharp set of **se**cateurs.

Katakana	English
曽 → ソ	SO

かきかた
ヽ ソ

おぼえかた
A **so**mbrero.

ソ
SO

Memory strategies

You have just learnt the first fifteen katakana.

- Have you been carefully following the stroke order as you write out each script?
- Have you been saying each katakana sound as you write out each script?
- Do you remember the pictures that go with each katakana?

D1

5

Lengthening a sound

A long horizontal line (ー) when writing horizontally, or a vertical line (l) when writing vertically, lengthens the sound.

Use the clues on the blackboard to help you identify each participant in this student forum.

Participants

Keith   Arthur

Sue   Casey

1

2

3

4

ケーシー

スー

キース

アーサー

D2

日本語について
にほんご

As you can see, English names and many other 'foreign' words can be written in Japanese by breaking the word into syllables and choosing the katakana that provides the closest sound. For example:

a Brisbane becomes ブリスベン.
bu ri su be n

b Kiss in English becomes キス in Japanese.
ki su

The 'u' is added because in Japanese the 's' sound cannot stand by itself. All consonants except 'n' must be followed by a 'vowel'.

c Hamburger becomes ハンバーガー.
ha n baa gaa

E₁ Extra sounds

Instead of having to learn a whole new katakana for every sound, sometimes you can add another symbol to a katakana you already know.

For example, if you add two short strokes to the top right-hand side of the 'カ' (ka) and 'サ' (sa) lines, different sounds are created as shown.

ザ za	サ sa	ガ ga	カ ka
ジ ji	シ shi	ギ gi	キ ki
ズ zu	ス su	グ gu	ク ku
ゼ ze	セ se	ゲ ge	ケ ke
ゾ zo	ソ so	ゴ go	コ ko

E₂ Making the 'n' sound

6

The katakana ン is very simple to write.

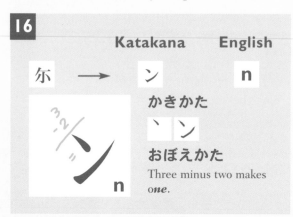

16

Katakana	English
尓 → ン	n

かきた
、 ン

おぼえかた
Three minus two makes o**ne**.

ガーデン カフェ

Garden Cafe

1F →

Which katakana can you now recognise in this sign?

F

Japanese elementary and junior high school students usually wear name badges similar to the one shown below. As you can see, their family name is the most important part of the badge.

Name of school:
Akita

Type of school:
Chuu gakkoo

Year level:
pronounced 'nen'

Family name:
Yamaguchi

Group:
pronounced 'kumi'

秋田　中学校
山　口
3年 2組

Can you work out who owns each of these three badges? What other information can you find out about each person?

Elementary School:
pronounced 'shoo gakkoo'

1

スーザン カー
インターナショナル スクール
マーズデン

2

アサクサ 小学校
6年 4組
タ カ ギ
エ ミ

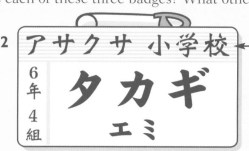

3

シドニー インターナショナル スクール
7年 A 組
ネイサン クリントン

6   Tsumiki I

The second set

	ワ wa	ラ ra	ヤ ya	マ ma	ハ ha	ナ na	タ ta	サ sa	カ ka	ア a
		リ ri		ミ mi	ヒ hi	ニ ni	チ chi	シ shi	キ ki	イ i
		ル ru	ユ yu	ム mu	フ fu	ヌ nu	ツ tsu	ス su	ク ku	ウ u
		レ re		メ me	ヘ he	ネ ne	テ te	セ se	ケ ke	エ e
ン n	ヲ o	ロ ro	ヨ yo	モ mo	ホ ho	ノ no	ト to	ソ so	コ ko	オ o

17

	Katakana	English
多 →	タ	**ta**

かきかた

ノ　ク　タ

おぼえかた

Use a ***tar***paulin to keep the firewood dry.

18

	Katakana	English
千 →	チ	**chi**

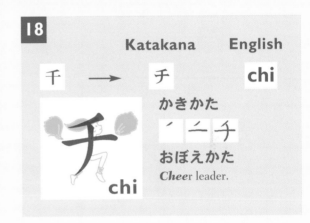

かきかた

ノ　ニ　チ

おぼえかた

Cheer leader.

19

	Katakana	English
川 →	ツ	**tsu**

かきかた

丶　丶丶　ツ

おぼえかた

Rugby Rat has a cold: 'Aah-***tsu***.'

20

	Katakana	English
天 →	テ	**te**

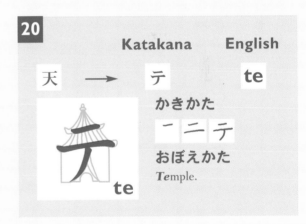

かきかた

一　二　テ

おぼえかた

Temple.

21

	Katakana	English
止 →	ト	**to**

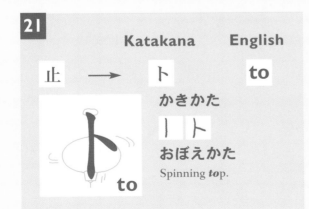

かきかた

丨　ト

おぼえかた

Spinning ***to***p.

22

	Katakana	English
奈 →	ナ	**na**

かきかた

一　ナ

おぼえかた

Bana***na***.

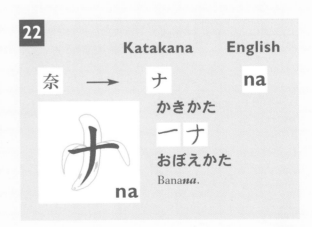

23

Katakana   English

二 → 二   **ni**

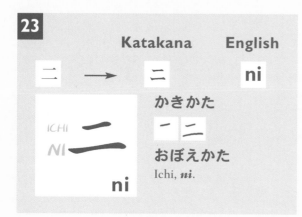

かきかた

一　二

おぼえかた

Ichi, *ni*.

24

Katakana   English

奴 → ヌ   **nu**

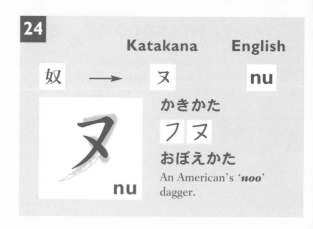

かきかた

フ　ヌ

おぼえかた

An American's '*noo*' dagger.

25

Katakana   English

祢 → ネ   **ne**

かきかた

、　ラ　ネ　ネ

おぼえかた

You can *ne*ver catch a pixie.

26

Katakana   English

乃 → ノ   **no**

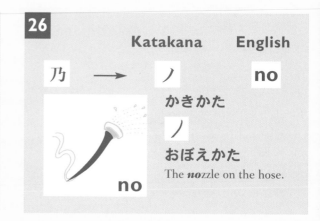

かきかた

ノ

おぼえかた

The *no*zzle on the hose.

27

Katakana   English

八 → ハ   **ha**

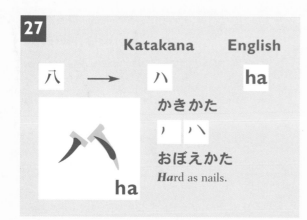

かきかた

ノ　ハ

おぼえかた

*Ha*rd as nails.

28

Katakana   English

比 → ヒ   **hi**

かきかた

一　ヒ

おぼえかた

*Hi*ps.

29

Katakana   English

不 → フ   **fu**

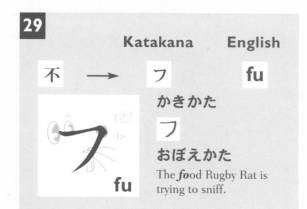

かきかた

フ

おぼえかた

The *fo*od Rugby Rat is trying to sniff.

30

Katakana   English

部 → ヘ   **he**

かきかた

ヘ

おぼえかた

*He*ad to the top of the mountain.

31

Katakana	English
保 → ホ	ho

かきかた
一 ナ オ ホ

おぼえかた
It's so **ho**t.

ホ
ho

What is this popular treat? (The picture provides the clue for reading the katakana correctly.)

G₂

8

Extra sounds

Two short strokes added to the ハ (ha) line creates the バ (ba) line. If a small circle is added to the ハ (ha) line, the パ (pa) line is created. Two short lines added to the タ (ta) line creates different sounds such as ダ (da).

ダ da	タ ta		パ pa	バ ba	ハ ha
ヂ ji*	チ chi		ピ pi	ビ bi	ヒ hi
ヅ zu*	ツ tsu		プ pu	ブ bu	フ fu
デ de	テ te		ペ pe	ベ be	ヘ he
ド do	ト to		ポ po	ボ bo	ホ ho

* These two are rarely used.

H

9

The katakana ツ gives the sound 'tsu', but it can be written at half its normal size and used to double the following consonant (except for 'n'). For example:

    sakkaa (soccer)   サッカー
    nokku (knock)   ノック

Can you work out what these words might be, and how they should be pronounced?

3 ホットケーキ

1 ホットドッグ

2 スパゲッティ

The third set

	ワ wa	ラ ra	ヤ ya	マ ma	ハ ha	ナ na	タ ta	サ sa	カ ka	ア a
		リ ri		ミ mi	ヒ hi	ニ ni	チ chi	シ shi	キ ki	イ i
		ル ru	ユ yu	ム mu	フ fu	ヌ nu	ツ tsu	ス su	ク ku	ウ u
		レ re		メ me	ヘ he	ネ ne	テ te	セ se	ケ ke	エ e
ン n	ヲ o	ロ ro	ヨ yo	モ mo	ホ ho	ノ no	ト to	ソ so	コ ko	オ o

32

Katakana   English

末 → マ   **ma**

かきかた

フ マ

おぼえかた

Ma's back is sore.

33

Katakana   English

三 → ミ   **mi**

かきかた

ヽ ミ ミ

おぼえかた

*Mi*ttsu (three).

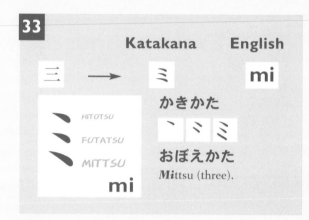

34

Katakana   English

牟 → ム   **mu**

かきかた

ノ ム ム

おぼえかた

*Mo*ve over.

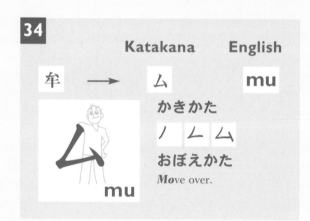

35

Katakana   English

女 → メ   **me**

かきかた

ノ メ

おぼえかた

Two roads have *me*t.

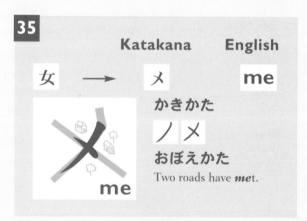

36

Katakana   English

毛 → モ   **mo**

かきかた

一 二 モ

おぼえかた

A *mo*th is attracted to the light.

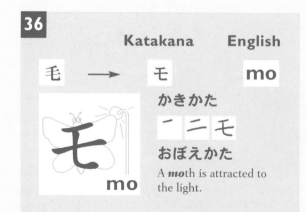

37

Katakana   English

也 → ヤ   **ya**

かきかた

フ ヤ

おぼえかた

*Ya*rn pulled through the crochet hook.

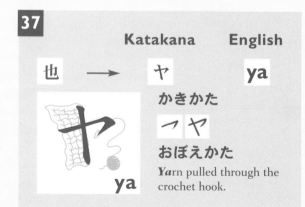

38

由 → ユ　　**yu**

Katakana　English

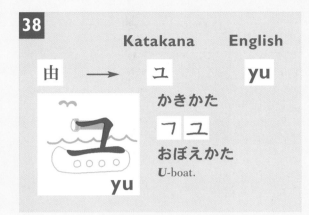

かきかた
フ　ユ

おぼえかた
U-boat.

ユ
yu

39

与 → ヨ　　**yo**

Katakana　English

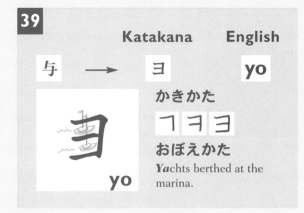

かきかた
フ　ヨ　ヨ

おぼえかた
*Ya*chts berthed at the marina.

ヨ
yo

40

良 → ラ　　**ra**

Katakana　English

かきかた
一　ラ

おぼえかた
*Ru*gby Rat with his *ru*gby ball.

ラ
ra

41

利 → リ　　**ri**

Katakana　English

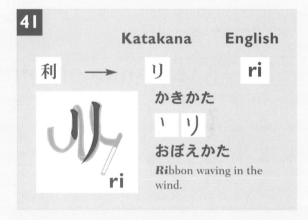

かきかた
ヽ　リ

おぼえかた
*Ri*bbon waving in the wind.

リ
ri

42

流 → ル　　**ru**

Katakana　English

かきかた
ヽ　ル

おぼえかた
Kanga*roo*'s strong back legs and tail.

ル
ru

43

礼 → レ　　**re**

Katakana　English

かきかた
レ

おぼえかた
*Re*cord player.

レ
re

44

呂 → ロ　　**ro**

Katakana　English

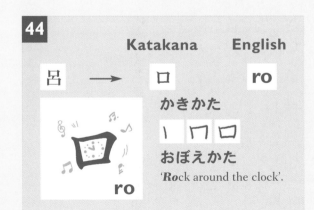

かきかた
｜　冂　ロ

おぼえかた
'*Ro*ck around the clock'.

ロ
ro

45

和 → ワ　　**wa**

Katakana　English

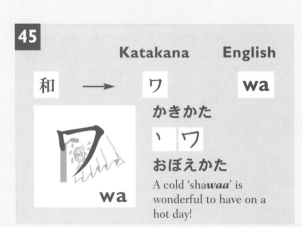

かきかた
ヽ　ワ

おぼえかた
A cold 'sha*waa*' is wonderful to have on a hot day!

ワ
wa

46

Katakana　English

乎　→　ヲ　　o

かきかた
フ ヲ

おぼえかた
An old *ox*.

You will rarely come across katakana ヲ except in telegrams and historical documents.

What is this sign telling you?

J₁ Katakana combinations

While trying to work out what this English children's song is, note the small ョ and see if you can work out how it is used.

ショールダーズ

ヘッド、　ショールダーズ、　ニーズ　アンド　トーズ、　ニーズ　アンド　トーズ。
ヘッド、　ショールダーズ、　ニーズ　アンド　トーズ、　ニーズ　アンド　トーズ
アンド　アイズ　アンド　イアズ　アンド　マウス　アンド　ノーズ。
ヘッド、　ショールダーズ、　ニーズ　アンド　トーズ、　ニーズ　アンド　トーズ。

J₂

12

By using a small ャ, ュ or ョ a greater variety of sounds can be made. Be careful to write the ャ, ュ or ョ half the size of the other katakana where they are used in combination with others, because the word will differ in meaning and pronunciation if you make them the same size. For example: キョウ (kyou) means 'today', while キヨウ (kiyou) means 'bulletin'.

ピャ pya	ビャ bya	ヒャ hya		ニャ nya		チャ cha		ジャ ja	シャ sha		ギャ gya	キャ kya
ピュ pyu	ビュ byu	ヒュ hyu		ニュ nyu		チュ chu		ジュ ju	シュ shu		ギュ gyu	キュ kyu
ピョ pyo	ビョ byo	ヒョ hyo		ニョ nyo		チョ cho		ジョ jo	ショ sho		ギョ gyo	キョ kyo

リャ rya	ミャ mya
リュ ryu	ミュ myu
リョ ryo	ミョ myo

J₃

These combined sounds can also be lengthened by adding the long line ー. For example:
コンピュータ　kompyuuta (computer)
ギョーザ　　　gyooza (Chinese dumpling)

Other katakana combinations for foreign words

As you have probably noticed by now, English words are not easily put into katakana. To try to make a more accurate sound for foreign words, katakana can be combined with a half-size vowel (ァa ィi ゥu ェe ォo) – as in the word 'fork' (フォーク).

These combined katakana have been created to make Japanese sounds mimic sounds from other languages. Some of these extra sounds and combinations are not used very often.

This chart shows some of these extra combined sounds for use in foreign words.

ファ fa		ツァ tsa			クァ kwa	
フィ fi	ティ ti					ウィ wi
フェ fe		ツェ tse	チェ che	シェ she		ウェ we	イェ ye
フォ fo		ツォ tso			クォ kwo	ウォ wo

ヴァ va				グァ gwa	
ヴィ vi	ディ di				
ヴ vu	デュ dyu				
ヴェ ve			ジェ je		
ヴォ vo					

Notice in the following words how the second katakana in a sound combination is written smaller to make the sound more closely copy the 'foreign' word.

1 フォ ーク   2 ディ ズニーランド   3 ファ ン

4 ウェ リントン   5 フィ ンランド

What is the name of this restaurant? What does it sell?

Note:
A dot (•) can be used to separate the parts of an expression written in katakana, or to make the katakana expression more meaningful.
For example:
エス・オー・エス (S.O.S)

L As we saw earlier, the 'long vowel' mark (ー) is written in the direction of the writing: vertically in vertical writing and horizontally in horizontal writing.

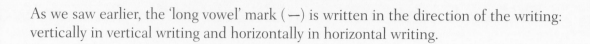

スカート   スカート

For words of Japanese origin, however, it is more common to lengthen the 'o' sound by adding 'u' (ウ).

Common names of plants and animals may be written in either hiragana or katakana. You will find lots of words of Japanese origin written in katakana in Japanese zoos or botanical gardens. Here are some examples of this use of ウ.

ダチョウ ostrich

コウモリ bat

コンゴウインコ macaw

コウノトリ stork

ゾウ elephant

フクロウ owl

ヒョウ leopard

Exception: オオカミ wolf

M Katakana stroke order

ハ ha	ナ na	タ ta	サ sa	カ ka	ア a
ヒ hi	ニ ni	チ chi	シ shi	キ ki	イ i
フ fu	ヌ nu	ツ tsu	ス su	ク ku	ウ u
ヘ he	ネ ne	テ te	セ se	ケ ke	エ e
ホ ho	ノ no	ト to	ソ so	コ ko	オ o

ワ wa	ラ ra	ヤ ya	マ ma
	リ ri		ミ mi
	ル ru	ユ yu	ム mu
	レ re		メ me
ン n	ヲ o	ロ ro	ヨ yo	モ mo

ひらがな
Hiragana

Outcomes
By the end of this unit, you should be able to:
• read and write hiragana both individually and in words.

A   The 46 basic hiragana

Just as every sound has a katakana equivalent, it also has a hiragana equivalent. Hiragana, like katakana, has 46 basic syllables, plus combination sounds and sounds that are made by adding two short strokes or a small circle to the basic hiragana. This chart provides an overview of the 46 basic hiragana and details of their stroke order.

は ha	な na	た ta	さ sa	か ka	あ a
ひ hi	に ni	ち chi	し shi	き ki	い i
ふ fu	ぬ nu	つ tsu	す su	く ku	う u
へ he	ね ne	て te	せ se	け ke	え e
ほ ho	の no	と to	そ so	こ ko	お o

わ wa	ら ra	や ya	ま ma
	り ri		み mi
	る ru	ゆ yu	む mu
	れ re		め me
ん n	を o	ろ ro	よ yo	も mo

You will be introduced to several hiragana at a time. Use the same techniques for learning hiragana as for katakana. Ways of using them in combinations will also be explained.

Try to learn the words listed below each hiragana. They will reinforce your memory of the hiragana and they will be useful to know once you start Unit 1 of this book.

The first set

わ wa	ら ra	や ya	ま ma	は ha	な na	た ta	さ sa	か ka	あ a
	り ri		み mi	ひ hi	に ni	ち chi	し shi	き ki	い i
	る ru	ゆ yu	む mu	ふ fu	ぬ nu	つ tsu	す su	く ku	う u
	れ re		め me	へ he	ね ne	て te	せ se	け ke	え e
ん n	を o	ろ ro	よ yo	も mo	ほ ho	の no	と to	そ so	こ ko	お o

1

Hiragana   English

於 → お   **o**

かきかた
‾ お お

おぼえかた
The golf ball is **o**n the green. お for **o**n.

ha yo u
おはよう   Good morning

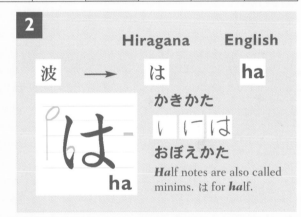

2

Hiragana   English

波 → は   **ha**

かきかた
い に は

おぼえかた
Half notes are also called minims. は for **ha**lf.

yo u
おはよう   Good morning

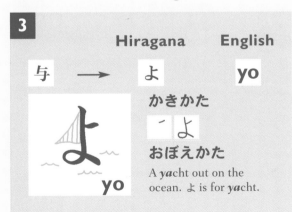

3

Hiragana   English

与 → よ   **yo**

かきかた
‾ よ

おぼえかた
A **ya**cht out on the ocean. よ is for **ya**cht.

おはよう   Good morning

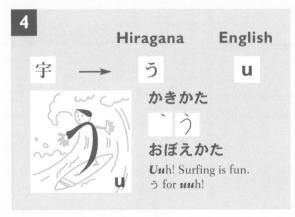

4

Hiragana   English

宇 → う   **u**

かきかた
` う

おぼえかた
Uuh! Surfing is fun. う for **uu**h!

u
おはよう   Good morning

Notice that the 'o' sound becomes longer when う is added. The long 'o' sound (sometimes written as 'oo' or 'ō') is pronounced the same as 'oar'.

5

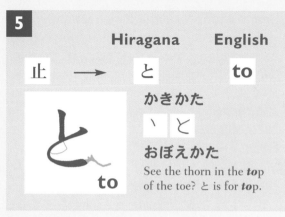

止 → と to

Hiragana **English**

かきかた
ヽ と

おぼえかた
See the thorn in the **to**p of the toe? と is for **to**p.

おとうさん [sa n] father
おとうと younger brother

6

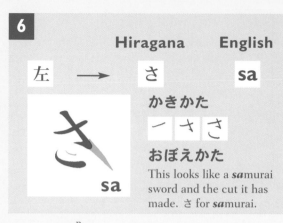

左 → さ sa

Hiragana **English**

かきかた
一 ナ さ

おぼえかた
This looks like a **sa**murai sword and the cut it has made. さ for **sa**murai.

おとうさん [n] father

7

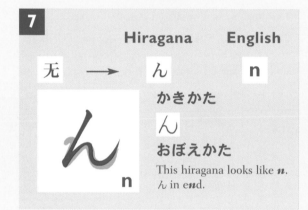

无 → ん n

Hiragana **English**

かきかた
ん

おぼえかた
This hiragana looks like **n**. ん in en**n**d.

おとうさん father
おばあさん [ba a] grandmother
おばさん [ba] aunty

8

加 → か ka

Hiragana **English**

かきかた
っ カ か

おぼえかた
Kicking a soc**cer** ball. か for soc**cer**.

おかあさん [a] mother
ありがとう [a ri ga] Thank you

Notice how 'ka' (か) changes to 'ga' by adding two short strokes (が).

9

安 → あ a

Hiragana **English**

かきかた
一 十 あ

おぼえかた
A cross on a grave. あ for **a**.

おかあさん mother
ありがとう [ri ga] Thank you

10

利 → り ri

Hiragana **English**

かきかた
ヽ り

おぼえかた
Reeds in the river. り for **ree**ds.

ありがとう [ga] Thank you
あり ant

Hiragana **English**

之 → し **shi**

かきかた
し

おぼえかた
The way *she* does her
hair. し for *she*.

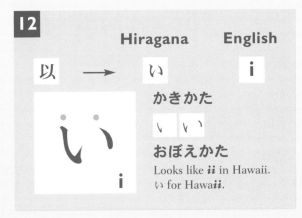

Hiragana **English**

以 → い **i**

かきかた
い い

おぼえかた
Looks like *ii* in Hawaii.
い for Hawa*ii*.

うし   cow
おじさん   uncle
おじいさん   grandfather

Notice how 'shi' (し) becomes 'ji' by adding two short
strokes (じ).

はい   yes
いい   good
あおい   blue
いもうと   younger sister

C

If this diagram is called a かけいず, what do you think a かけいず is called in English? Draw
a simple かけいず that applies to you or your friend.

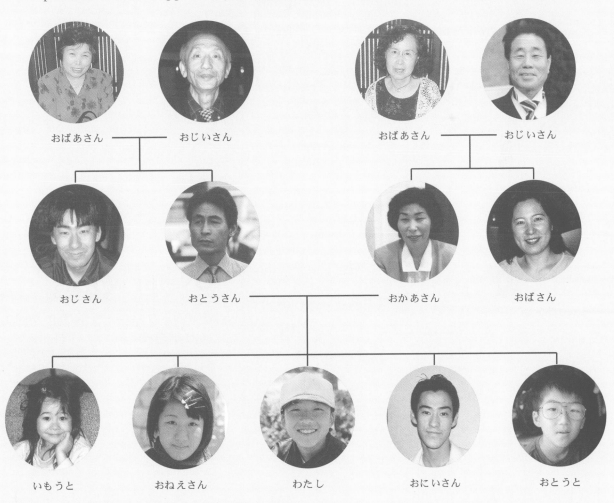

おばあさん —— おじいさん   おばあさん —— おじいさん

おじさん   おとうさん —— おかあさん   おばさん

いもうと   おねえさん   わたし   おにいさん   おとうと

If you are labelling someone else's family tree, you should add さん to いもうと and
おとうと.

The second set

	wa	ra	ya	ma	ha	na	ta	sa	ka	a
	わ wa	ら ra	や ya	ま ma	は ha	な na	た ta	さ sa	か ka	あ a
		り ri		み mi	ひ hi	に ni	ち chi	し shi	き ki	い i
		る ru	ゆ yu	む mu	ふ fu	ぬ nu	つ tsu	す su	く ku	う u
		れ re		め me	へ he	ね ne	て te	せ se	け ke	え e
ん n	を o	ろ ro	よ yo	も mo	ほ ho	の no	と to	そ so	こ ko	お o

13

幾	→	Hiragana き	English ki

かきかた
一 二 キ き

おぼえかた
A **ke**y and lock.
き for **ke**y.

き ki

かぎ (gi)   key
きく (ku)   chrysanthemum
うさぎ (gi)   rabbit

Sound changes

Notice how the 'k' sound changes to a 'g' sound by simply adding two short strokes.

が ga	か ka
ぎ gi	き ki
ぐ gu	く ku
げ ge	け ke
ご go	こ ko

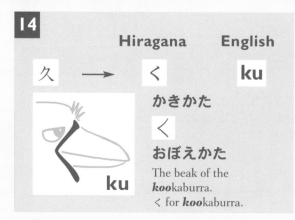

14

久	→	Hiragana く	English ku

かきかた
く

おぼえかた
The beak of the **koo**kaburra.
く for **koo**kaburra.

く ku

かぞく (zo)   family
こくばん (ko)(ba)   blackboard

Useful words

かがく　　　　　　　　Chemistry
ありがとう　　　　　　Thank you
おはようございます　Good morning

15

Hiragana **English**

計 → け **ke**

かきかた
い | に | け

おぼえかた
A *ke*ttle full of hot water.
け for *ke*ttle.

けん	Ken (*an abbreviated version of several Japanese male names*)
けんいち [chi]	Kenichi (*a boy's name*)
けんたろう [ta ro]	Kentaroo (*a boy's name*)

17

Hiragana **English**

寸 → す **su**

かきかた
一 | す

おぼえかた
A plant which has a new leaf, roots and a seed below the ground. *Soo*n there'll be a new flower. す for *soo*n.

いただきます [ta da ma]	I humbly receive this food (*Said before eating*)
すき	like

19

Hiragana **English**

曽 → そ **so**

かきかた
そ

おぼえかた
そ looks like a baby's *so*ck.
そ for *so*ck.

ごちそうさまでした [chi] [ma de]	Thank you for the wonderful meal (*Said at the end of a meal*)
かぞく	family

16

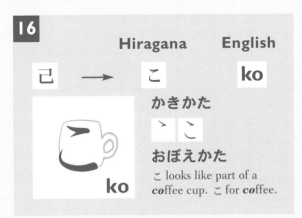

Hiragana **English**

己 → こ **ko**

かきかた
丶 | こ

おぼえかた
こ looks like part of a *co*ffee cup. こ for *co*ffee.

こくばん [ba] blackboard

18

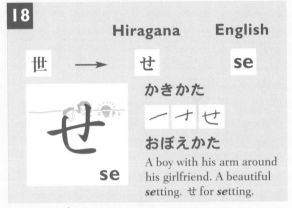

Hiragana **English**

世 → せ **se**

かきかた
一 | 十 | せ

おぼえかた
A boy with his arm around his girlfriend. A beautiful *se*tting. せ for *se*tting.

いらっしゃいませ [ra] [sha] [ma] Welcome
(*Said by shop assistants as you enter a shop*)

Sound changes

Notice how the 's' sound changes to a 'z' sound by adding the two short strokes.

ざ za	さ sa
じ ji	し shi
ず zu	す su
ぜ ze	せ se
ぞ zo	そ so

Useful words

ぞう	elephant
ねずみ [ne] [mi]	mouse, rat
おはようございます [ma]	Good morning
おじいさん	grandfather
おじさん	uncle

20

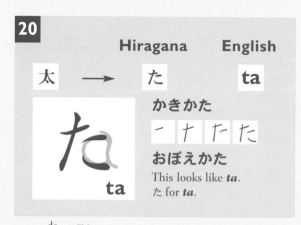

太 → た **ta**

Hiragana　**English**

かきかた
一 ナ た た

おぼえかた
This looks like **ta**.
た for **ta**.

いただきます　I humbly receive this food
da　*ma*

Notice how た (ta) is changed to だ (da) by adding two short strokes.

21

称 → ね **ne**

Hiragana　**English**

かきかた
↓ ね

おぼえかた
A hole in a basketball **ne**t.
ね for **ne**t.

ねこ　　　cat
おねえさん　older sister
e

22

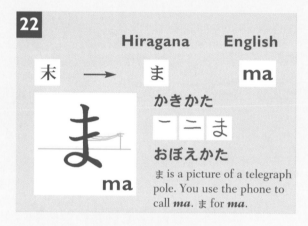

末 → ま **ma**

Hiragana　**English**

かきかた
一 二 ま

おぼえかた
ま is a picture of a telegraph pole. You use the phone to call **ma**. ま for **ma**.

たまご　　egg
ただいま　I'm home!

23

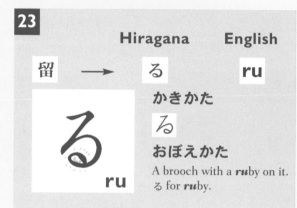

留 → る **ru**

Hiragana　**English**

かきかた
る

おぼえかた
A brooch with a **ru**by on it.
る for **ru**by.

うるさい　noisy
いるか　　dolphin
さる　　　monkey

24

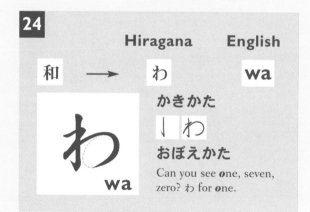

和 → わ **wa**

Hiragana　　**English**

かきかた
↓ わ

おぼえかた
Can you see **o**ne, seven, zero? わ for **o**ne.

わたし　　　I, me
わあ！　　　Wow!
わに　　　　crocodile
ni

Memory strategies

- Have you been copying out each hiragana carefully, following the stroke order given?　☑

- Have you made yourself a little set of hiragana cards so that you can check if you still remember each hiragana you have learnt?　☑

- How many words can you now write in hiragana?　**10+** ☑

The third set

わ wa	ら ra	や ya	ま ma	は ha	な na	た ta	さ sa	か ka	あ a
	り ri		み mi	ひ hi	に ni	ち chi	し shi	き ki	い i
	る ru	ゆ yu	む mu	ふ fu	ぬ nu	つ tsu	す su	く ku	う u
	れ re		め me	へ he	ね ne	て te	せ se	け ke	え e
ん n	を o	ろ ro	よ yo	も mo	ほ ho	の no	と to	そ so	こ ko	お o

25

知 → ち chi

Hiragana   English

かきかた
一 ち

おぼえかた
A **chee**se-ball with a fancy toothpick. ち for **chee**se.

ごちそうさまで^{de}した   Thank you for this wonderful meal

ちず   map

26

川 → つ tsu

Hiragana   English

かきかた
つ

おぼえかた
A Japanese sneeze. っ for **tsu**.

つくえ^e   desk
いつ   when
つみ^{mi}き   building blocks
つき   moon

27

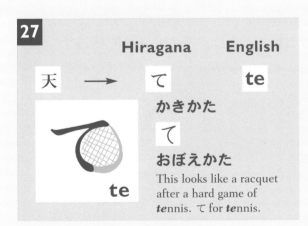

天 → て te

Hiragana   English

かきかた
て

おぼえかた
This looks like a racquet after a hard game of **te**nnis. て for **te**nnis.

てあらい   toilet, washroom
て   hand

Sound changes

だ da	た ta
ぢ ji*	ち chi
づ zu*	つ tsu
で de	て te
ど do	と to

The 'ta' sound, too, is easily changed to 'da' by adding the two short strokes.

* These two are rarely used.

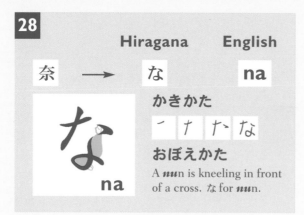

28

Hiragana **English**

奈 → な na

かきかた
ー ナ 左 な

おぼえかた
A **nu**n is kneeling in front of a cross. な for **nu**n.

なし	Japanese pear
なな	seven
しんじられない	I can't believe it!
なまたまご	raw egg

(ra re above じられ)

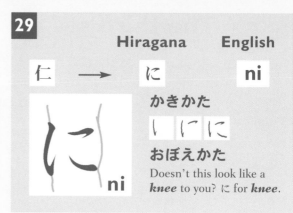

29

Hiragana **English**

仁 → に ni

かきかた
い に に

おぼえかた
Doesn't this look like a **knee** to you? に for **knee**.

にほん	Japan
おにいさん	older brother
にわ	garden

(ho above にほ)

30

Hiragana **English**

乃 → の no

かきかた
の

おぼえかた
A **kno**t in a rope. の for **kno**t.

| のみます | I drink |
| のぞみ | a super fast 'bullet train' |

(mi above のみ and のぞみ)

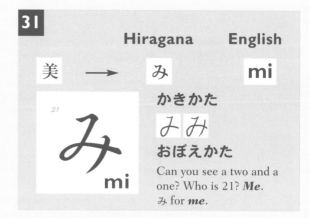

31

Hiragana **English**

美 → み mi

かきかた
み み

おぼえかた
Can you see a two and a one? Who is 21? **Me**. み for **me**.

たたみ	tatami (mats)
みち	street
みます	I see
みぎ	right (side)

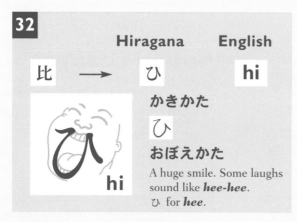

32

Hiragana **English**

比 → ひ hi

かきかた
ひ

おぼえかた
A huge smile. Some laughs sound like **hee-hee**. ひ for **hee**.

ひま	time, spare time
ひみつ	secret
びじゅつ	art
ひなまつり	Doll Festival

(bi ju above びじゅつ)

33

Hiragana **English**

不 → ふ fu

かきかた
丶 う ふ ふ

おぼえかた
Mt **Fu**ji is a volcano. ふ for **Fu**ji.

ふじさん	Mt Fuji
ぶんか	culture
ふね	ship, boat

(bu above ぶんか, ne above ふね)

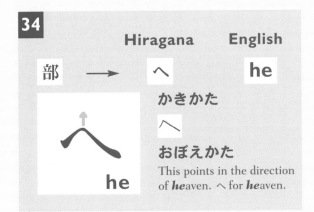

34

部 → へ **he**

Hiragana   English

かきかた
へ

おぼえかた
This points in the direction of **he**aven. へ for **he**aven.

べんごし (be) lawyer
ふべん (be) inconvenient
おべんとう (be) packed lunch

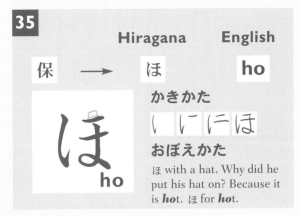

35

保 → ほ **ho**

Hiragana   English

かきかた
ー に に ほ

おぼえかた
ほ with a hat. Why did he put his hat on? Because it is **ho**t. ほ for **ho**t.

たんぽぽ (po po) dandelion
にっぽん (ni po n) Japan

E₂

ぱ pa	ば ba	は ha
ぴ pi	び bi	ひ hi
ぷ pu	ぶ bu	ふ fu
ぺ pe	べ be	へ he
ぽ po	ぼ bo	ほ ho

Sound changes

The 'ha' sound can be changed in two ways. By adding two short strokes the 'ba' sound is made. Adding a small circle creates the 'pa' sound. Other hiragana can be changed in the same way, as this table shows. See how it works in the following words:

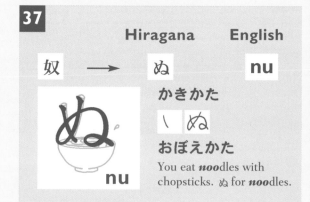
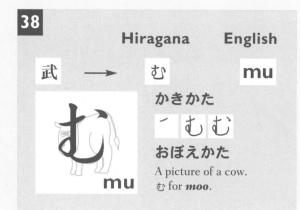

F

9

The fourth set

	wa	ra	ya	ma	ha	na	ta	sa	ka	a
	わ wa	ら ra	や ya	ま ma	は ha	な na	た ta	さ sa	か ka	あ a
		り ri		み mi	ひ hi	に ni	ち chi	し shi	き ki	い i
		る ru	ゆ yu	む mu	ふ fu	ぬ nu	つ tsu	す su	く ku	う u
		れ re		め me	へ he	ね ne	て te	せ se	け ke	え e
ん n	を o	ろ ro	よ yo	も mo	ほ ho	の no	と to	そ so	こ ko	お o

36

衣 → え　**e**

Hiragana　English

かきかた
、え

おぼえかた
ん with an *e*xtra dot and a line. え for *e*xtra.

えき	railway station
えん	yen
ふえ	flute

37

奴 → ぬ　**nu**

Hiragana　English

かきかた
ぬ

おぼえかた
You eat *noo*dles with chopsticks. ぬ for *noo*dles.

いぬ	dog
ぬいぐるみ	stuffed toy or doll
こいぬ	puppy

38

武 → む　**mu**

Hiragana　English

かきかた
ー む む

おぼえかた
A picture of a cow. む for *moo*.

むかし	long ago
むら	village
むずかしい	difficult

39

女 → め　**me**

Hiragana　English

かきかた
、ぬ

おぼえかた
When you drop the egg from the egg noodles it becomes *me*ssy. め for *me*ssy.

はじめに	firstly
めがね	spectacles

40

Hiragana   English

毛 → も   **mo**

かきかた
し も も

おぼえかた
A *mo*p that is dripping wet.
も for *mo*p.

もみじ   maple (tree)
もも   peach
もり   forest
いもうと   younger sister

41

Hiragana   English

也 → や   **ya**

かきかた
つ つ や

おぼえかた
The tree is in the back
*ya*rd. や for *ya*rd.

やぎ   goat
やきそば   fried noodles with
           vegetables and meat
やま   mountain

42

Hiragana   English

由 → ゆ   **yu**

かきかた
ゆ ゆ

おぼえかた
No *u*-turn in Japan.
ゆ for *u*-turn.

ゆ   hot water
ゆび   finger

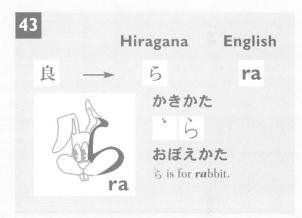

43

Hiragana   English

良 → ら   **ra**

かきかた
、 ら

おぼえかた
ら is for *ra*bbit.

らくだ   camel
らくがき   scribbling, graffiti

44

Hiragana   English

礼 → れ   **re**

かきかた
れ

おぼえかた
A mountain climber
*re*sting on his walking
stick. れ for *re*sting.

れいぞうこ   refrigerator
れきし   history

See how the name of this town is given in kanji,
hiragana and English so that everyone can read it.

45		Hiragana	English
呂 →		ろ	ro

かきかた ろ

おぼえかた
A **ro**bber takes the ruby.
ろ for **ro**bber.

ろく   six
おふろ   bath

46		Hiragana	English
袁 →		を	o

かきかた 一 ち を

おぼえかた
An **A**ustralian **O**lympic discus thrower. を for **A**ustralian and **O**lympic.

This hiragana is not used in words but it is an essential hiragana used when constructing sentences.

G₁ Combination sounds

Many combination sounds can be made by combining a small や or ゆ or よ with certain hiragana. These combination sounds are shown below.

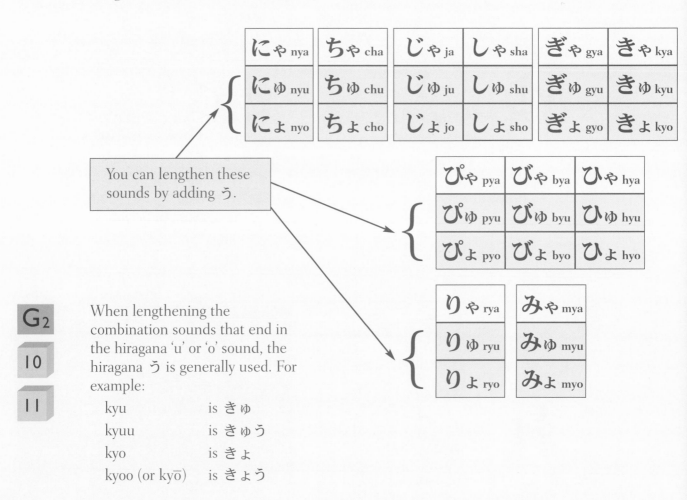

You can lengthen these sounds by adding う.

にゃ nya	ちゃ cha	じゃ ja	しゃ sha	ぎゃ gya	きゃ kya
にゅ nyu	ちゅ chu	じゅ ju	しゅ shu	ぎゅ gyu	きゅ kyu
にょ nyo	ちょ cho	じょ jo	しょ sho	ぎょ gyo	きょ kyo

ぴゃ pya	びゃ bya	ひゃ hya
ぴゅ pyu	びゅ byu	ひゅ hyu
ぴょ pyo	びょ byo	ひょ hyo

りゃ rya	みゃ mya
りゅ ryu	みゅ myu
りょ ryo	みょ myo

G₂
10
11

When lengthening the combination sounds that end in the hiragana 'u' or 'o' sound, the hiragana う is generally used. For example:

kyu   is きゅ
kyuu   is きゅう
kyo   is きょ
kyoo (or kyō)   is きょう

'Farewell/goodbye'

Useful words that follow this rule include:

べんきょう	study	れんしゅう	practice
じょうず	skilful	おとうさん	father
おとうと	younger brother	そうです。	That/It is so./Yes, that's right.

There are a few exceptions to this rule, such as:

おおさか	Osaka
とお	ten
おおきい	big

The sounds あ 'a', い 'i' and え 'e' are lengthened by adding あ, い or え respectively. For example:

おか_{ka}あさん	mother
おに_{ni}い_iさん	older brother
おね_{ne}え_eさん	older sister

H

12

13

14

I

When doubling consonants other than 'n' and 'm', the rule is simple. Replace the first of the double consonants with a small っ. For example:

がっこう	ga**kk**oo	school		にっぽん	ni**pp**on	Japan
にっき	ni**kk**i	diary				

J

When 'n' and 'm' are doubled, they are not treated as above. Instead, the hiragana ん is used as shown below:

みんな	mi**nn**a	everyone		どんな	do**nn**a	What kind of …

As you work through this book, you may find it necessary to come back to this unit regularly to check that you are writing each hiragana correctly.

It will be useful to keep a copy of page 16 handy so that you have a ready reference as you embark on the next stage of your language journey. You can also refer to the hiragana chart on the inside front cover.

1 わたし
Me

Outcomes
By the end of this unit, you should be able to:
- introduce yourself to others
- provide others with information about yourself – your name, your nationality and where you live
- seek information from others by asking questions about the above
- use basic conversational greetings
- understand some frequently used classroom instructions.

A₁ Andrew McDonald, from Sydney, Australia, and Mariana Allen, from Auckland, New Zealand, are two young students of Japanese. They are both planning to go to Japan for several weeks. They already know a few words and they are keen to learn as much as they can before they go.

アンドルーさんの会話

一 みなさん、おはようございます。わたしは せんせいです。

二 オーストラリアじんです。シドニーに すんでいます。あなたは？

三 わたしは アンドルー マクドナルドです。オーストラリアじんです。シドニーに すんでいます。

四 アンドルーさん、ありがとうございます。

1	わたし	I/me	7	…です	I am/It is …
2	アンドルーさんの会話	Andrew's conversation	8	オーストラリアじん	Australian
3	みなさん	everyone	9	シドニー	Sydney
4	おはようございます	Good morning	10	…に すんでいます	I/You live in …
5	わたしは	I (the subject of the sentence)	11	あなたは？	(What about) you?
6	せんせい	teacher	12	アンドルー マクドナルド	Andrew McDonald
			13	ありがとうございます	Thanks (very much)

マリアナさんの会話

1	マリアナさんの 会話	Mariana's conversation	
2	こんにちは	Hello	
3	おなまえは？	What is your name?	
4	マリアナ　アレン	Mariana Allen	
5	ニュージーランドじん	New Zealander	

6	オークランドの グリーンベイ	Green Bay, Auckland
7	あ、ベルです	Oh! That's the bell
8	また　あした	See you again tomorrow
9	ありがとう ございました	Thank you very much (for what you have done)

覚えましょう
Introductions

> 覚えましょう means 'Let's memorise this'. This heading appears above new sentence patterns to remind you that you should try to learn them by heart.

Sentence pattern 1

Q	おなまえは？	What is your name?
A	（わたしは）アンドルーです。	I am Andrew.

Sentence pattern 2

Q	なまえは　なんですか。	What is his/her name?
A	アンドルー　マクドナルドさんです。	He is Andrew McDonald.
A	すずき　えみこさんです。	She is Emiko Suzuki.

Explanation

1 Brackets (…) around words in a sentence pattern show that those words are optional – you do not have to use them.

2 さん is an honorific title and is used in Japan instead of Mr, Mrs, Miss or Ms. It is used to show respect to other people. You never use it when referring to yourself.

B 2

You may not know everyone in your class. Introduce yourself to the class, then ask another person what their name is. Continue around the class.

 This kanji, pronounced れい, means 'example'. It is used to provide a model for completing an activity.

わたしは
アンドルー
マクドナルドです。
おなまえは？

わたしは　ダイアン　ホークです。

おなまえは？

日本語について

In Japanese, 'I' and 'you' are not used as frequently as in English. Once you have been introduced to someone, you should try to remember their name and use it instead of 'you'.

日本語について

Young children are often given the title ~ちゃん instead of ~さん. Young boys frequently use ~くん among their friends.

1 なん　　　　　　　what
2 ダイアン　ホーク　Dianne Hawke

Young children often call their close friends by their nicknames or first names followed by the suffix ~ちゃん. As children get older, however, it becomes more common to use their family name. By senior high school, young people are addressed by their family name. Adults and work colleagues would use family names when speaking to each other.

In society at large, people who have titles are addressed with their title (alone, or attached to their name)—for example, やまだせんせい or simply せんせい. It would be considered very impolite to address such people with their family name followed by さん.

When introducing themselves to another person, Japanese put their family name first, followed by their first name. When Japanese people use foreign names, such as Dianne Hawke, they generally put the family name last, following the convention of the nation from which the name comes. So they would usually say ダイアン　ホーク. Similarly, Andrew would give his first name first.

わたしは　すずき
としゆきです。

C Names

Family names

5 Japanese family names are more important than first names and are used more commonly, even among friends. You need to be familiar with some of the common Japanese family names, such as those below, so that you can repeat and remember them with ease when you are introduced to a Japanese person. Getting your tongue around some of them can be quite tricky!

さとう「佐藤」

すずき「鈴木」

たかはし「高橋」

いとう「伊藤」

わたなべ「渡辺」

さいとう「斎藤」

たなか「田中」

こばやし「小林」

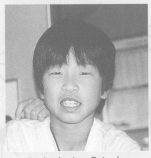
やまもと「山本」

やまだ「山田」

Most westerners point to
their chest when referring to
themselves, but Japanese
point to their nose.

Family names/surnames

Not until 1875 were Japanese required by law to have a surname.
They took whatever surname they wanted. Some used the names
of fish because they were fishermen. Others took names
representing locations or occupations.

They made up the names by combining kanji to give a desired
meaning, for example:

田中	Tanaka	In the paddy fields
山田	Yamada	Paddy fields in/near the mountains
中村	Nakamura	Middle of the village

As a result there are more family names in Japan today than in
any other country in the world. There are probably more than
130,000 different names in Japan, compared with about 50,000
in the USA and Europe combined.

In Japan, with a population of some 120 million, there are about
2 million people with the name Sato, about 2 million Suzukis and
up to 1.3 million Takahashis. The next most common names in
descending order of frequency are Ito, Watanabe, Saito, Tanaka,
Kobayashi, Sasaki and Yamamoto.

D
6
7

First names

These Japanese boys and girls have commonly used names. Like given names in any other
culture, certain names become trendy for a period of time. You might like to find out the
current most popular names by asking your Japanese friends or searching the Web.

あきこ

たけし

きょうこ

あきら

ゆうこ

みちこ ゆきこ あいこ

しんじ

つよし としお

けんすけ かずゆき

覚えましょう
Nationalities

ちゅうごくじんです。

Sentence pattern

3

Q （あなたは）にほんじんですか。   Are you Japanese?

A はい、にほんじんです。   Yes, I'm Japanese.

A いいえ、ちゅうごくじんです。   No, I'm Chinese.

| Nationality | + | です。| I am/You are (nationality).

Explanation

1 Note how か changes a statement into a question.

2 In this course, わたし and あなた are used to mean 'I' and 'you' respectively. Among their school friends, boys may like to use ぼく for 'I' and きみ for 'you'. However, it is much better (as you read on page 32) to use a person's name if you know it, rather than あなた or きみ. Neither is considered polite if you know the person's name. わたしは is often omitted at the beginning of a sentence if it is clear that you are talking about yourself.

3 To tell somebody what nationality you are or what nationality somebody else is, all you do is add じん, which means person, to the name of the country from which you or the other person comes. For example, オーストラリア means 'Australia' and オーストラリアじん is 'an Australian'.

書きましょう

書きましょう means 'Let's write' and heads sections that introduce kanji.

8

Instead of writing two hiragana to identify your nationality (じ plus ん), you might find it easier and quicker to write just one simple kanji: 人.

人 is pronounced じん and means 'person', so オーストラリア人 means 'an Australian'. Use the stroke order shown below when writing it.

くん and おん refer respectively to the Japanese and Chinese readings (or way of pronouncing) kanji. Examples of how you can use the kanji are listed next to れい (example). As each kanji in *Tsumiki* is introduced, the vocabulary item that you are expected to know at this stage is highlighted in green.

Try to remember a kanji by associating it with a picture and a story. The picture shows how the kanji developed over time, slowly changing to make it simple and faster to write.

1 **person**

かきかた (stroke order)

ノ 人

なりたち (history/origin)

It is easy to see that this character represents a person. The pronunciation is じん.

おん	にん、じん
くん	ひと
れい	オーストラリア人

Australian (person)

1 いいえ   no   3 ちゅうごくじん Chinese (person)
2 にほんじん   Japanese (person)

Countries and nationalities

Apart from Japan, China, Korea and Taiwan, country names are written in katakana.
Look at the nationalities shown on this world map. When talking about someone's
nationality, add 人 to the name of the country from which they come.

こくせきは? is an easy way to ask what country a person comes from. To answer, you only need to say what country you come from. You can reinforce it by adding your nationality.

こくせきは？

にほんです。
にほん人です。

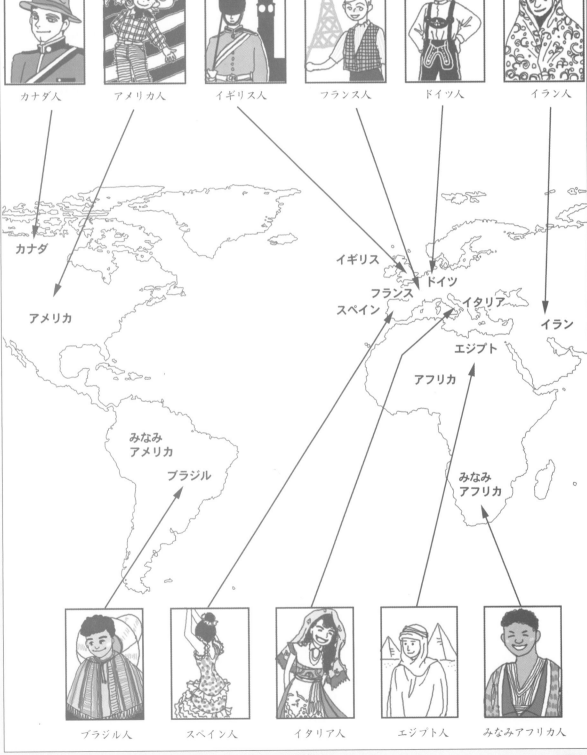

カナダ人

アメリカ人

イギリス人

フランス人

ドイツ人

イラン人

カナダ

イギリス

ドイツ

フランス

イタリア

スペイン

アメリカ

イラン

エジプト

アフリカ

みなみ
アメリカ

ブラジル

みなみ
アフリカ

ブラジル人

スペイン人

イタリア人

エジプト人

みなみアフリカ人

覚えましょう
Where do you live?

Sentence pattern

4

Q どこに すんでいますか。 — Where do you live?
A にほんに すんでいます。 — I live in Japan.
or A こうべに すんでいます。 — I live in Kobe.

| Place + に | + | verb すんでいます。 | I/You live in/at (place)

or A にほんの こうべに すんでいます。 — I live in Kobe, which is in Japan.

or A こうべの すみよしに すんでいます。 — I live in Sumiyoshi, which is an area of Kobe.

Explanation

1 どこ is a question word meaning 'where?', as in '**Where** do you live?' and '**Where** are you going?' As with English, it is not repeated in the answer.

2 Some verbs always require a certain 'sign' or 'meaning marker' in front of them. すんでいます is one of those verbs. You always put に before すんでいます when explaining where you live or where someone else lives. In English, we say 'I live **in** Adelaide' or 'I live **at** Manly'. The に before すんでいます has the same function and meaning as 'in' or 'at' when talking about where you live or where someone else lives.

3 If you want to be very specific about where you live, use the pattern shown in the last two examples in the sentence pattern above.

| Larger area + の | + | Smaller area + に | + | すんでいます。

日本語について

In *Tsumiki* the meaning markers have been attached to the preceding part of the sentence because they add meaning to it.

Spaces have been inserted to indicate a completely different phrase or word.

This is the style of print generally adopted in Japan in books for children.

In adult literature, no spaces are used at all. While learning Japanese, you may find it helpful to insert the spaces, as has been done in this book, to help you understand the structure of the language.

Text from a children's book

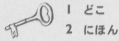

1 どこ — where
2 にほん — Japan

38 Tsumiki 1

Text from a magazine for adults

In a Japanese sentence, if you want to talk about a specific person, the person's name plus は is put at the beginning of the sentence. So when you want to say where a particular person lives, follow the pattern:

| Person's name + は | + | place where person lives + に | + | すんでいます。 |

Using the information given, write sentences saying where the following people live. An example has been done for you.

例　マリアナ　アレンさんは　オークランドに　すんでいます。

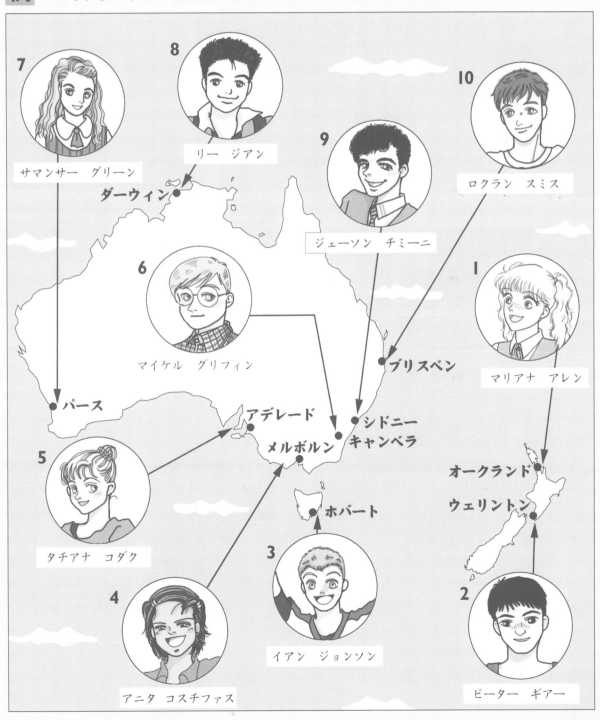

歌いましょう
Let's sing!

(To the tune of 'Frère Jacques')

「おはよう」
おはよう、おはよう
こんにちは、こんにちは
さようなら、さようなら
また　あした、また　あした

Classroom instructions

14

15

During your Japanese lessons, your teacher will use lots of Japanese phrases that you may not have learnt. These are some of the most useful.

1	どうぞ　はいって　ください。	Please come in.
2	かいて　ください。	Please write.
3	もういちど　いって　ください。	Please say it once more.
4	ノートを　あけて　ください。	Please open your notebooks.
5	しずかに。	Be quiet!
6	すわって　ください。	Please sit down.
7	たって　ください。	Please stand up.

日本語について

In spoken language, Japanese do not use さようなら as an all-purpose equivalent of 'Goodbye'. When wishing to say 'See you later', or 'Goodbye', it's probably better to say じゃ、また. The expression さようなら is only used in a few situations. You might say it to your teacher at the end of the last lesson of the day, or if you see your teacher in the corridor after school.

At the end of a normal lesson, a class monitor would say きりつ、れい！ (Stand up and bow!) After this formal close, no more greetings are exchanged.

At the beginning of a lesson, the monitor would call the class to order with きりつ、れい。ちゃくせき！(Stand up, bow. Sit!).

If you were at an airport and wanted to say 'Goodbye', you would use the expression いってらっしゃい, which means something like 'Go and please come back'. The person leaving would say いってきます (I'm going and I shall come back).

1	さようなら。	Goodbye, farewell.
2	じゃ、また。	Well, see you again.
3	いってらっしゃい。	Goodbye. (Literally: Go and please come back)
4	いってきます。	See you again. (Literally: I'm going and I shall come back)

Putting it all together

Mariana frequently visits a chat room on the Internet. She was thrilled when somebody from Japan wrote this little note. There were only a couple of words that she had not learnt, but she was able to guess what this person said.

Are you able to understand the message?

セルフ テスト

Here is a short quiz for you to check your understanding of the main content of this unit. If you have any trouble, go back and review the relevant sentence pattern.

1 おなまえは？

2 どこに すんでいますか。

3 にほん人ですか。

4 アルバート アインシュタインさんは イギリス人ですか。

5 ブリスベンの マンリーに すんでいますか。

 Memory strategy
(Literally: How to remember)

At the end of each unit, spend some time completing the セルフ テスト. If you don't know something, go back over that sentence pattern and/or vocabulary. Every week go back over all the セルフ テスト of previous units so that you don't forget anything.

2 かず
Numbers

Outcomes

By the end of this unit, you should be able to:
- count to 99 and write these numbers in kanji
- give your own age and the age of others
- inform others about your year level at school
- say and write telephone numbers
- make a simple 'business card'.

A1

We use numbers all the time when we communicate with others. In providing more information about themselves to their Japanese friends, Andrew and Mariana use numbers frequently. In the following conversations they continue to get to know the Japanese visitors to their schools.

アンドルーさんの会話

1	なんねんせい ですか	What year are you in at school?	6	じゅうさんさい	thirteen years of age
2	いちねんせい	first year student	7	じゅうにさい	twelve years of age
3	はちねんせい	year 8 student	8	ようこさんの でんわばんごう	Yoko's telephone number
4	え？	What?	9	なんばんですか	What number is it?
5	なんさいですか	How old are you?	10	…の	…'s (possessive)

マリアナさんの会話

Counting

Before you can say someone's age, you need to know the basic Japanese numbering system. Japanese use different counters depending on what they are counting (such as cars, animals, pencils and ages). However, once you know the basic numbers it is easy to make the slight adjustments necessary so that you can count anything.

Study the basic numbers on the left and see how, with a minor adjustment, you can create the counter for ages. Notice that the kanji for 20 years of age is different. You are not expected to write this age in kanji at this stage.

	BASIC NUMBERS		AGES	
	Pronunciation	Kanji	Pronunciation	Kanji
1	いち	一	いっさい	一才
2	に	二	にさい	二才
3	さん	三	さんさい	三才
4	よん、し	四	よんさい	四才
5	ご	五	ごさい	五才
6	ろく	六	ろくさい	六才
7	なな、しち	七	ななさい	七才
8	はち	八	はっさい	八才
9	きゅう、く	九	きゅうさい	九才
10	じゅう	十	じゅっさい	十才
11	じゅういち	十一	じゅういっさい	十一才
12	じゅうに	十二	じゅうにさい	十二才
13	じゅうさん	十三	じゅうさんさい	十三才
14	じゅうよん、じゅうし	十四	じゅうよんさい	十四才
20	にじゅう	二十	はたち	二十歳
21	にじゅういち	二十一	にじゅういっさい	二十一才
30	さんじゅう	三十	さんじゅっさい	三十才
32	さんじゅうに	三十二	さんじゅうにさい	三十二才
40	よんじゅう	四十	よんじゅっさい	四十才
50	ごじゅう	五十	ごじゅっさい	五十才
60	ろくじゅう	六十	ろくじゅっさい	六十才
70	ななじゅう	七十	ななじゅっさい	七十才
80	はちじゅう	八十	はちじゅっさい	八十才
90	きゅうじゅう	九十	きゅうじゅっさい	九十才
99	きゅうじゅうきゅう	九十九	きゅうじゅうきゅうさい	九十九才

In some cases, Japanese use arabic numerals for their numbers instead of kanji. Prices, telephone numbers, numbers in addresses and ages are generally written in arabic notation.

Mr Tanaka's business card shows that he, like many other older people, still prefers to write the numbers in kanji (the Chinese script). Yoko Matsuda, on the other hand, has had her business card printed using arabic numerals.

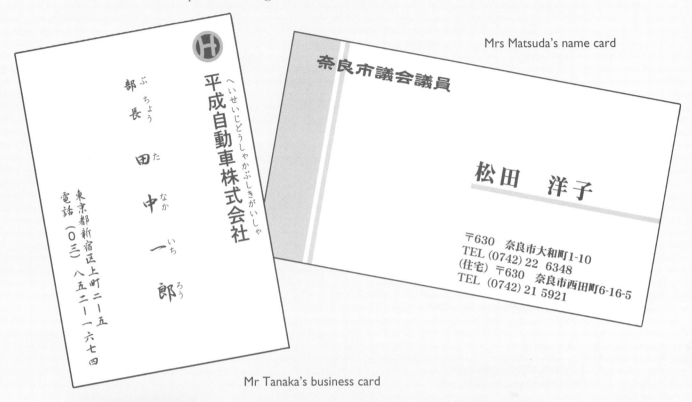

Mrs Matsuda's name card

奈良市議会議員

松田　洋子

〒630　奈良市大和町1-10
TEL (0742) 22　6348
(住宅) 〒630　奈良市西田町6-16-5
TEL (0742) 21 5921

平成自動車株式会社
（へいせいじどうしゃかぶしきがいしゃ）

部長
（ぶちょう）

田中一郎
（た　なか　いち　ろう）

東京都新宿区上町二一五
電話（０三）八五二一一六七四

Mr Tanaka's business card

日本について（にほん）

Name cards/business cards — めいし

While westerners try to find out what a person is like and what his or her job is, Japanese like to know each other's social position and for which company their new acquaintance works. The easiest way of getting this information is via the めいし or name card.

めいし are exchanged printed side up and accepted in the right hand while bowing slightly. Once the contents have been read, you bow again. めいし should be treated respectfully and so should not be shoved into your pocket or purse and should not be written on.

Nowadays めいし are printed with Japanese on one side as shown, and sometimes with the details written in English on the other side. One's name and business position are printed in the centre of the card, with the address and phone number on the left, as on Mr Tanaka's card. These days, however, many めいし adopt quite different layouts and styles.

Arabic numerals are a great help if your knowledge of kanji is limited! How much does this bowl of tempura udon cost?

天ぷらうどん　宮島
¥750

覚え方

Whichever system you use to write numbers (arabic numerals, hiragana or kanji), you still need to know how to **say** the number. While you are still learning hiragana and trying to perfect your pronunciation, it is a good idea to continue to write out the whole number in hiragana.

Arabic numeral	Kanji	Hiragana
1 (pronounced いち)	一 (pronounced いち)	いち (pronounced and written as いち)
2 (pronounced に)	二 (pronounced に)	に (pronounced and written as に)
3 (pronounced さん)	三 (pronounced さん)	さん (pronounced and written as さん)

日本について

Just as some westerners are superstitious about the number 13, some Japanese worry about the consequences of using number 4. 'Four' can be pronounced し or よん. Also pronounced し is the word for 'death'. Therefore, you may find Japanese hotels with no room 4.

覚えましょう

Age

Sentence pattern

5a

Q	(あなたは) なんさいですか。	How old are you?
A	(わたしは) じゅうさんさいです。	I am 13 years of age.

Sentence pattern

5b

Q	おかあさんは　なんさいですか。	How old is your mother?
A	おかあさんは　よんじゅっさいです。	Mum is 40 years old.

Person + は + Number + さい + です。　(*Person*) is … years of age.

Explanation

If you want to ask about a specific person's age, simply put:

The person's name + は + なんさいですか。

as shown in the sentence pattern above.

は is a 'meaning marker'. Japanese use these markers or じょし to:

* give **meaning** to the sentence
* **mark** particular parts of the sentence.

'Meaning markers' point backwards to something or someone. は tells you who or what is the topic or subject of the sentence. Your sentences can take on different meanings by using different meaning markers. You will see how this happens as you progress through this course.

C₂ Age is expressed in different ways in these twelve sentences. What differences can you find?

1 としおくんは　いっさいです。

2 まりこちゃんは　にさいです。

3 さんさいです。

4 わたしは　よんさいです。

5 ぼくは　ごさいです。

6 ぼくは　ろくさいです。

7 ぼくは　はっさいです。

8 わたしは　きゅうさいです。

9 じゅっさいです。

10 おとうとは　じゅうにさいです。

11 わたしは　じゅうさんさいです。

12 おとうさんは　さんじゅうななさいです。

1	ぼく	I, me (used by boys)
2	おとうと	younger brother
3	おとうさん	father

書^かきましょう

Once you learn how to **say** the numbers and ages perfectly, and when you can write them perfectly in hiragana, you can then try to write them in kanji. It is certainly much quicker!

2 one

かきかた (stroke order)

なりたち (history/origin)

When you are pointing to one person it is easy to see how the kanji for 'one' evolved.

おん	ひと (つ)
くん	いち
れい	一人 one person 一 one

3 two

かきかた

なりたち

In indicating two things, we can still see the kanji for 'two'.

おん	に
くん	ふた (つ)
れい	二 two, 二人 two people

4 three

かきかた

なりたち

You can still see the kanji when indicating three objects.

おん	さん
くん	み、みっ (つ)
れい	三 three, 三時 three o'clock

5 four

かきかた

なりたち

A simple way to remember this kanji is that a window with a curtain in it has four sides.

おん	し
くん	よん、よ、よっ(つ)
れい	四 four, 四才 four years of age

6 five

かきかた

なりたち

The number five began in a similar way to one, two and three, with each line representing one unit. But, as there were too many horizontal lines, the Chinese eventually turned two of the lines vertically and chopped off a corner so that it looked balanced.

おん	ご
くん	いつ (つ)
れい	五 five

7 six

なりたち

Here is a student sitting at a desk at school for six hours a day.

かきかた

`、 ー ナ 六`

おん	ろく
くん	む、むい、むっ（つ）
れい	六 six， 六日 sixth day of the month

8 seven

なりたち

Five fingers and two make seven.

かきかた

`ー 七`

おん	しち
くん	なの、なな（つ）
れい	七 seven， 七 seven

9 eight

なりたち

Four plus four is eight (4 + 4 = 8).

かきかた

`ノ 八`

おん	はち
くん	やっ（つ）、よう
れい	八 eight， 八日 eighth day of the month

10 nine

なりたち

After practising the kanji for the numbers one to nine you will have developed great strength.

かきかた

`ノ 九`

おん	きゅう、く
くん	ここの（つ）
れい	九 nine， 九 nine， 九つ nine

11 ten

なりたち

There are ten fingers on two crossed hands.

かきかた

`ー 十`

おん	じゅう
くん	とお、と
れい	十 ten

12 age, talent

なりたち

Talent increases with age, just as the seedling grows taller as it is nurtured. This kanji is much easier to remember than the full form 歳.

かきかた

`ー ナ 才`

おん	
くん	
れい	さい 十三才 thirteen years of age

Ages of other people

Mariana has added to her photo album a section just for her friends from Japan. She has been practising her kanji. Can you work out

- whose photos she has included, and
- her friends' ages?

2 すずき りえさんは 十一才 です。

3 たなか としさんは 十四才です。

1 おかもと えみさんは 十三才です。

4 たなか りょうへいさんは 十五才です。

5 さとう ゆうこさんは 十六才です。

6 かしはら あやのさんは 十二才です。

7 せとぐち しんくんは 八才です。

8 かとう けんじさんは 十九才です。

Useful expressions

In English we have a variety of expressions which we use when introducing ourselves and so do the Japanese. Compare these two sets of introductions:

Adults (formal)

I am Keiji Nakamura.

How do you do. (I'm very pleased to meet you.)

I'm pleased to meet you too. (The pleasure is all mine.)

Children (very informal)

I am Toshio Watanabe.

I am Sonoe Suzuki.

(I'm) glad to meet you.

I'm glad to meet you (too).

G1

覚えましょう

Sentence pattern

6a

Q （あなたは）なんねんせいですか。 — What year/grade are you in at school?

A はちねんせいです。 — I am in year 8.

| School grade ＋ ねんせい | ＋ | です。 | — I am in year …

Explanation

ねん means 'year'. せい means 'student'. Together, these two words mean 'a student in year …'

<ruby>覚<rt>おぼ</rt></ruby>えましょう
Year of schooling

If you or your Japanese friends wish to make it very clear which level of school you are in—for example, first year of junior high school (or middle school) or second year of senior high school—it is best to use the following pattern.

Sentence pattern

6b

Q （あなたは）なんねんせいですか。 — What year/grade are you in at school?

A ちゅうがっこうの　いちねんせいです。 — I'm in first year of middle school.

Not only is their year at school important to Japanese children, so too is the group to which they belong, as indicated on these labels for books and pencils.

名前　なまえ (name)
年　　ねん (year)
組　　くみ (group, class)

<ruby>覚<rt>おぼ</rt></ruby>えましょう
Telephone numbers

Telephones, especially mobile phones, are fast replacing letter-writing as the tool for teenage communication. Fortunately, it is very easy to express telephone numbers in Japanese.

Sentence pattern

7

Q （ようこさんの）でんわばんごうは
なんばんですか。 — What is your (Yoko's) telephone number?

A でんわばんごうは　ゼロにの
ごきゅうろくよんの　ににさんはちです。 — The telephone number is 02 5964 2238.

A わたしの　でんわばんごうは　ゼロにの
ごきゅうろくよんの　ににさんはちです。 — My telephone number is 02 5964 2238.

Explanation

1 If Japanese want to express ownership they use the meaning marker の. Although it is much like …'s in English, it has other uses that make it very useful. For instance, to change 'I' (わたし) to 'my', you simply add の. わたしの　でんわ　ばんごう means 'my telephone number'.

2 Notice the use of の when expressing the actual telephone number. Wherever we put a space in an English telephone number, Japanese say の. However, you do not include the の when writing down a telephone number.

1	しょうがっこう	elementary school	
2	ちゅうがっこう	middle school/junior high school	
3	こうとうがっこう	senior high school (abbrev. こうこう)	
4	でんわばんごう	telephone number	

Whose telephone numbers have been listed in Mariana's diary, and what are they?

1 すずき　けいじさんの　でんわばんごうは　〇九〇の　三四四六の　二二九八　です。

2 やきた　みえこさんの　でんわばんごうは　〇九〇の　二三六一の　一三五二　です。

3 ダイアン　ヤングさんの　でんわばんごうは　〇七の　八四三六の　二三三一　です。

The following pages from the Internet use arabic numerals in addresses, telephone numbers, faxes and costs.

• Can you work out the telephone or fax area code for Tokyo?

• Calculate the dollar value for a twin room for one night at the cheapest rate. (You will need to check the paper for today's exchange rate.)

J

Times tables

Japanese children are encouraged from a young age to know their tables. A popular 'toy' is the 'Digital Multiplier', which helps children learn their tables off by heart. Each table is reduced to just a few syllables so that children can remember them. See how you go learning these tables in Japanese. The が is often deleted to reduce the number of syllables in the longer phrases. This makes it easier and faster to learn.

2 × table

2 × 1 = 2	にいちがに
2 × 2 = 4	ににんがし
2 × 3 = 6	にさんがろく
2 × 4 = 8	にしがはち
2 × 5 = 10	にごがじゅう
2 × 6 = 12	にろくじゅうに
2 × 7 = 14	にしちじゅうし
2 × 8 = 16	にはちじゅうろく
2 × 9 = 18	にくじゅうはち

3 × table

3 × 1 = 3	さんいちがさん
3 × 2 = 6	さんにがろく
3 × 3 = 9	さざんがく
3 × 4 = 12	さんしじゅうに
3 × 5 = 15	さんごじゅうご
3 × 6 = 18	さんろくじゅうはち
3 × 7 = 21	さんしちにじゅういち
3 × 8 = 24	さんはちにじゅうし
3 × 9 = 27	さんくにじゅうしち

K

セルフ テスト

14

15

Can you answer the following questions?

1　なん才ですか。

2　なんねんせいですか。

3　でんわばんごうは　なんばんですか。

4　てつやさんは　なん才ですか。

5　アンドルーさんは　なんねんせいですか。

6　てつやさんの　でんわばんごうは　なんばんですか。

7　ちゅうがっこうの　三ねんせいですか。

8　がっこうの　でんわばんごうは　なんばんですか。

9　おとうさんは　なん才ですか。

10　マリアナさんは　しょうがっこうの　二ねんせいですか。

3 ともだち
Friends

Outcomes

By the end of this unit, you should be able to:
- provide and seek information about sports, games and musical instruments played, and languages learnt
- comment on your skill at various activities
- greet friends appropriately
- write simple self-introductory letters
- search websites for information.

A1

When young people meet for the first time, they usually try to find common ground. They talk about what they like doing, their hobbies and sports. Here Andrew and Mariana discuss these topics with their Japanese visitors.

アンドルーさんの会話（かいわ）

としおくん、どんな
スポーツを　しますか。

サッカーを　します。

アンドルーくんは
サッカーを　しますか。

いいえ、クリケットと
バスケットボールを　します。
としおくんは　からてを
しますか。

ええ、でも…
へたです。

1	ともだち	friend	7	… と …	… and … (in a list)
2	どんな	what, what kind of	8	バスケット ボール	basketball
3	スポーツ	sports	9	からて	karate
4	… します	I/You do/play …	10	ええ	yeah
5	サッカー	soccer	11	でも	but, however
6	クリケット	cricket	12	へた	poor, weak at something

マリアナさんの会話

一　まいさん、ピアノを　ひきますか。

二　いいえ、ひきません。でも　バイオリンを　ひきます。マリアナさんは？

三　ピアノを　ひきます。まいさんは　どんな　スポーツを　しますか。

四　バスケットボールを　します。マリアナさんは？

五　たっきゅうを　します。まいさんは　えいごを　ならっていますか。ええ、でも…へたです。

六　マリアナさんは　にほんごが　じょうずですね！いいえ、そんなことは　ないです。

1	ピアノ	piano
2	… ひきます	I/You play … (the piano, guitar, violin)
3	バイオリン	violin
4	たっきゅう	table tennis
5	えいご	English
6	… ならっています	I/You learn (am/are learning) …
7	にほんご	Japanese language
8	じょうず	skilful, good at something
9	にほんごが じょうずですね	You're good at Japanese, aren't you?
10	いいえ、そんな ことはないです。	No, that is not so./No, not at all. (A polite way of saying 'I'm not very good!')

覚えましょう

Playing sport and games

Sentence pattern

8a

Q どんな スポーツを しますか。　What (kind of) sports do you do/play?

A やきゅうを します。　I play baseball.

Sentence pattern

8b

Q やきゅうを しますか。　Do you play baseball?

A はい、やきゅうを します。　Yes, I play baseball.

A いいえ、たっきゅうを します。　No, I play table tennis.

Explanation

1 The main verb in any Japanese sentence always goes at the end of the sentence.

2 Usually the verb します means 'do'. Here, referring to sports, it means 'play'.

3 If you can ask 'what?' of your verb (e.g. **What** do you play?) and find an answer in the sentence, then the thing that you are doing or playing is called the object of the sentence. Thus, in the sentence 'I play baseball':

a Ask 'what?' of your verb. Ask '**What** do you play?'

b Is there an answer to that question in the sentence? Yes, 'baseball' answers that question.

c So 'baseball' is the object of the sentence. The meaning marker that points to the object is を.

B₂

日本について

じゅうどう

Judo is a traditional Japanese sport in which wrestlers use techniques of throwing and grappling to overcome the opponent.

日本について

けんどう

Kendo is another traditional Japanese sport. It is a form of fencing in which the opponents wear face masks and chest guards to protect themselves from the poles that each fencer wields. The object is to try to strike the opponent's mask or chest.

| 1 | やきゅう | baseball |

日本語について

Two hiragana are pronounced 'o': お and を. お is used in words such as おかあさん. を is only used as a meaning marker.

日本について
からて
Karate came to Japan from China as a martial art in which opponents attempt to overpower each other by using various kicking and punching techniques.

日本について
すもう
Sumo is a traditional sport in which two wrestlers face each other in a ring. The first wrestler to bring his opponent to the ground or to push him out of the ring is the winner.

日本について
やきゅう
Baseball is probably the most popular sport in Japan. Games are broadcast on TV almost daily during the baseball season (April–October). It was introduced to Japan in 1872 by two Americans. There are two professional baseball leagues in Japan.

日本について
サッカー
Soccer is also a very popular sport among children as well as adults. It increases in popularity year by year, especially since the establishment in 1993 of the professional league called J-league.

日本について
あいきどう
Aikido is a modern non-competitive and non-violent martial art in which the person develops strength of mind and body.

日本について
じゃんけん
Janken ('paper, scissors and rock') is a traditional children's game played as a way of deciding who wins something or who goes first.

日本について
けんだま
Kendama is a traditional toy game in which the player attempts to flip a ball into a holder.

日本について
しょうぎ
Shogi is a board game similar to chess in that the object is to capture the opponent's king.

Western sports are written in katakana. However, baseball, swimming, gymnastics and table tennis have a kanji equivalent so they can be written in hiragana. Traditional sports, obviously, are also written in hiragana or kanji.

How do you say that you play or do each of these sports or activities?

| 1 サッカー (Jリーグ) | 2 テニス | 3 ボクシング | 4 レスリング | 5 スキー |

| 6 スケート | 7 バスケットボール | 8 ホッケー | 9 りくじょう | 10 たいそう |

| 11 ゴルフ | 12 セーリング | 13 フットボール | 14 バレーボール | 15 すいえい |

| 16 じゅうどう | 17 からて | 18 けんどう | 19 あいきどう | 20 すもう |

1 テニス	tennis	7 りくじょう	track and field	12 バレーボール	volleyball
2 ボクシング	boxing			13 すいえい	swimming
3 レスリング	wrestling	8 たいそう	gymnastics	14 じゅうどう	judo
4 スキー	skiing	9 ゴルフ	golf	15 けんどう	kendo
5 スケート	skating	10 セーリング	sailing	16 あいきどう	aikido
6 ホッケー	hockey	11 フットボール	football	17 すもう	sumo

覚えましょう

Sentence pattern

9

a　としおさんは　テニスを　します。　Toshio plays tennis.

b　まいさんは　スキーを　します。　Mai skis.

Explanation

1　The verb します does not literally mean 'play'. In fact it means 'do'. One 'does' tennis, 'does' skiing and 'does' baseball.

2　As in the previous sentence patterns, if you want to say who is playing a particular sport, simply follow this pattern:

| Name of person + は | + | sport + を | + | verb します。 |

Who plays what sports in these illustrations?

1　ジョンさんは　サッカーを　します。

2　マクドナルドさんは　からてを　します。

3　マリアナさんは　たっきゅうを　します。

4　としおさんは　けんどうを　します。

5　けんすけさんは　やきゅうを　します。

6　まいさんは　バレーボールを　します。

C₃ Games

Japanese children play a range of other games, both traditional and western. Sentence pattern 9 is also used in telling someone you play these games. Which of these do you play?

1 なわとびを　します。

2 じゃんけんを　します。

3 おりがみを　します。

4 チェスを　します。

5 コンピュータゲームを　します。

6 しょうぎを　します。

7 カルタを　します。

8 マージャンを　します。

9 けんだまを　します。

1	なわとび	skipping; rope jumping	5	コンピュータ ゲーム	computer games
2	じゃんけん	janken (rock, scissors, paper)	6	しょうぎ	Japanese chess
3	おりがみ	origami (paper folding)	7	カルタ	traditional Japanese playing-cards
4	チェス	chess	8	マージャン	mah-jong
			9	けんだま	traditional game (ball on a string)

Musical instruments

To explain to someone that you play a particular musical instrument, you can use the basic structures of sentence patterns 8 and 9 but with more appropriate verbs.

Strings

ピアノ
ギター 　　　　を　ひきます。(to pluck)
バイオリン

Woodwind

フルート
オーボエ 　　　を　ふきます。 (to blow)
クラリネット

Percussion

たいこ 　　　　を　うちます。　(to beat)

Brass

トランペット
　　　　　　　を　ふきます。(to blow)
サックス

Note: The verb ひきます is used to talk about playing a piano, even though the strings in the piano are not actually plucked.

日本について

Music, whether it is studying an instrument, playing in a band, listening to CDs or watching music videos, is a popular pastime among Japanese young people. They enjoy a wide variety of music such as rock, hip hop, reggae, eurobeat and techno pop, including hits from the United States and the United Kingdom.

Karaoke (meaning 'empty orchestra') is popular throughout Japan and helps ensure the continued popularity of particular songs.

1	... ひきます	I/You (will) play ... (a musical instrument: pluck)	7	フルート	flute
2	... ふきます	I/You (will) play ... (a musical instrument: blow)	8	オーボエ	oboe
3	... うちます	I/You (will) play ... (a musical instrument: beat)	9	クラリネット	clarinet
4	ピアノ	piano	10	たいこ	Japanese-style drums
5	ギター	guitar	11	トランペット	trumpet
6	バイオリン	violin	12	サックス	saxophone

Foreign languages

In Japanese, there is a strong link between the name of a country, the name of the people who live there, and the word for the language spoken in that country. With the exception of English (えいご), the word for the language of the country is usually formed by simply adding ご to the name of the country. (Note: this does not always apply. For example, in Australia we speak えいご and in New Caledonia people speak フランスご.)

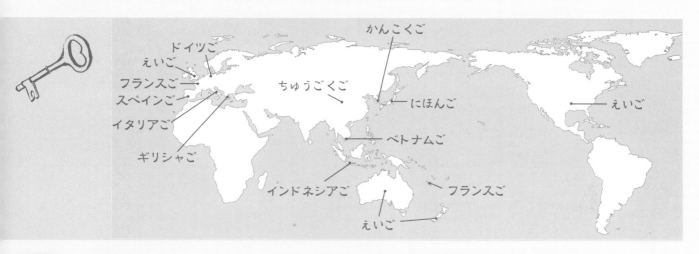

E2

覚えましょう

If you wish to tell someone what you are learning, the pattern is the same as sentence patterns 7a and 7b, except that, instead of using します (I do or I will do), you use ならっています (I **am** learn**ing**). As always in a Japanese sentence, the verb or action word comes last.

Sentence pattern

10

Q	にほんごを　ならっていますか。	Do you learn Japanese?/ Are you learning Japanese?
A	はい、にほんごを　ならっています。	Yes, I am learning Japanese.
A	いいえ、にほんごを ならっていません。	No, I don't learn Japanese./ I am not learning Japanese.

Explanation

You can change any sentence into a negative statement by changing す to せん. This works for all verbs, so you can now say what it is that you are **not** learning, **don't** do and **don't** play. It might help you to remember that 'do **n**ot' contains the '**n**' sound. So too does the Japanese equivalent, せ**ん**.

フランスごを　ならっていません。	I am not learning French.
ピアノを　ひきません。	I don't play the piano.
チェスを　しません。	I don't play chess.
たっきゅうを　しません。	I don't play table tennis.

Useful expressions—more greetings

We often ask friends 'How are you?' It is almost a greeting like 'Good day'. The Japanese, however, usually reserve the spoken usage of 'How are you?' for occasions when they really want an answer—for example, when they have not seen someone for a long time.

Q How are you?
A I'm well, thanks. And what about you, Mrs Suzuki?

A I'm well, thanks.

おげんきですか
is a common question at the beginning of a letter, just as it is in English letter-writing. Read this letter that Andrew received from his new friend Kensuke.

After studying the layout and greetings used, write a reply to Kensuke.
Use correct setting out and expressions to answer Kensuke's questions.
Ask questions of your own, using similar patterns to those that Kensuke used.
(You should be able to work out the meaning of any new words.)

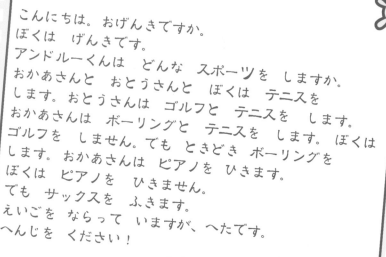

アンドルーくんへ

こんにちは。おげんきですか。
ぼくは　げんきです。
アンドルーくんは　どんな　スポーツを　しますか。
おかあさんと　おとうさんと　ぼくは　テニスを
します。おとうさんは　ゴルフと　テニスを　します。
おかあさんは　ボーリングと　テニスを　します。ぼくは
ゴルフを　しません。でも　ときどき　ボーリングを
します。おかあさんは　ピアノを　ひきます。
ぼくは　ピアノを　ひきません。
でも　サックスを　ふきます。
えいごを　ならって　いますが、へたです。
へんじを　ください！

さようなら

けんすけより

1 ... へ	to ... (at the beginning of a letter)	3 へんじを　ください　Please reply
2 ... が	but, however	4 ... より　from ... (at the end of a letter)

G1 Praising someone's skill

日本語について

Japanese like to praise a person's skill as a way of demonstrating their genuine friendship with that person. It is a way of encouraging the listener in whatever he or she is doing, and it also shows that the speaker wants to deepen his or her friendship with the listener. Thus Japanese people will compliment a student of Japanese on the quality of his or her Japanese language very soon after meeting that person.

On the other hand, it is polite to be humble in your response. It would be very rude to brag about your talents, even if you are very good at something. For example, Japanese people frequently begin formal speeches (that they have taken a long time to prepare) with an apology for the poor quality of the speech about to be delivered, even though it is probably very good.

G2 Useful expressions

15

The following expressions are handy to know when you wish to compliment Japanese friends on their English or other skills, and as you respond to their comments about your standard of Japanese or your standard of skill in some other activity.

Wow, you are very good at it, aren't you!
(Literally: Wow! You are very skilful, aren't you!)

No, it's not (good) yet/I'm still not good at it.

My name is Terri Smith. I live in Wellington in New Zealand.

Your Japanese is very good, isn't it!

It's not really!

1 まだまだ   not yet ... (I'm still not good at it, I still have much more to learn.)
2 ... ね   ... isn't it/aren't you

Personal profiles

Andrew has started filling in the forms for his trip to Japan. Like you, he probably would need a dictionary to look up some of the words; others he can guess. What new information about him have you discovered?

せいと 生徒のデータ		
	なまえ 名前	Andrew McDonald アンドルー マクドナルド
	じゅうしょ 住所	8 Simpson Street Manly Sydney Australia
	ゆうびんばんごう 郵便番号	② ⓪ ⓪ ③
	でんわばんごう 電話番号	02 3424 6983
		E メールアドレス　mcdonald.a@globe.au
	がっこう 学校	Manly High School マンリー ハイスクール
	なんねんせい 何年生ですか。	２ねんせい
	なんさい 何才ですか。	13才

に ほん ご 日本語	●に ほん ご 日本語を ならっていますか。　はい ☑ いいえ ☐

どのくらい？

ねんかん
1年間 |∨____|____|____|____|____| ねんかん
5年間
　　　　1　　　2　　　3　　　4　　　5

レベルは？

|___✕___|_____|_____|
へた　　　　　　まあまあ　　　　じょうず

スポーツ	●どんな スポーツを しますか。 　クリケットと バスケットボール をします。

がっき 楽器	●がっき 楽器を ならっていますか。　はい ☑ いいえ ☐

☐ピアノ　☐フルート　☐サックス　☑ギター, オーボエ

アレルギー	●リスト　ペニシリン 　　　　　　　　クローバー はい　　いいえ　チョーク ☐　　　☐

| た
その他 | コンピュータ ゲームを します。 |

セルフ　テスト

1　どんな　スポーツを　しますか。

2　ピアノを　ひきますか。

3　にほんごを　ならっていますか。

4　おとうさんは　テニスを　しますか。

5　おかあさんは　クラリネットを　ふきますか。

6　How would you reply if someone said the following to you?

    a　こんにちは。

    b　おはようございます。

    c　にほんごが　じょうずですね。

7　リー　フンさんは　ちゅうごく人ですか。

8　にほん人は　クリケットを　しますか。

<ruby>覚<rt>おぼ</rt></ruby>え<ruby>方<rt>かた</rt></ruby>

Have you checked the self-tests in Units 1 and 2 recently? Now would be a good time to revise the first three units.

4 がっこう
School

Outcomes

By the end of this unit, you should be able to:
- share information about school subjects that you study or do not study
- express likes and dislikes
- share information by email.

A1

As Andrew and Mariana talk with their Japanese friends, they are able to compare school life in Japan with their Australian or New Zealand experiences. As you read or hear the dialogues, take note of the similarities and the differences between the Japanese educational experience and your own.

アンドルーさんの会話（かいわ）

1	がっこうで	at school	
2	なに	what	
3	べんきょうして います	I/You study, I am/You are studying	
4	すうがく	Mathematics	
5	や	and … (so on)	
6	こくご	National Language (Japanese)	

7	りか	Science
8	いちばんすきなかもく	favourite subject
9	すきです	I like
10	すきじゃないです	I don't like
11	ほんとう	Really? Is that right?
12	おなじですね	It's the same (for both of us), isn't it?

A₂ # マリアナさんの会話（かいわ）

一
> マリアナさん、じゅぎょうの あとで ピアノを ひきますか。

> いいえ、じゅぎょうの まえに ピアノを ひきます。

二
> おんがくが すきですか。

> はい、すきです。

三
> いちばんすきな かもくは おんがく ですか。

> いいえ、すうがくです。

四
> ほんとうですか。

> まいさんは コンピュータを ならっていますか。

> ほんとうです！

五
> いいえ、がっこうで コンピュータを ならっていません。

六
> まいさん、えいごを べんきょうしていますか。

> はい、もちろん。ともだちは みんな えいごを べんきょうしています。

1	じゅぎょうの あとで	after lessons (after school)	4	もちろん	of course
2	じゅぎょうの まえに	before lessons (before school)	5	みんな	everyone
3	おんがく	Music	6	ともだち	friend

The education system in Japan

Compare your education system with that in Japan. What similarities and differences are there?

日本について

Organisation of the Japanese school system

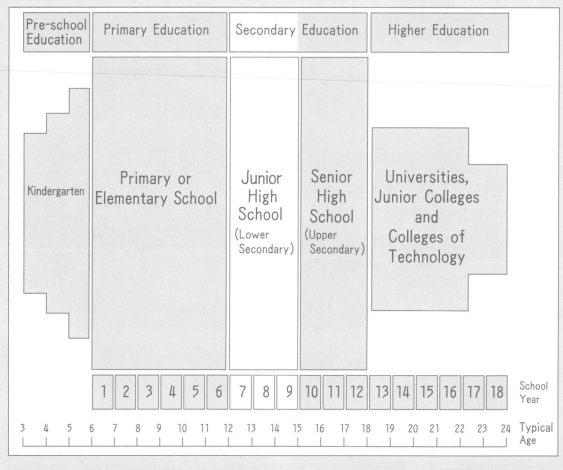

Pre-school Education	Primary Education	Secondary Education	Higher Education
Kindergarten	Primary or Elementary School	Junior High School (Lower Secondary) / Senior High School (Upper Secondary)	Universities, Junior Colleges and Colleges of Technology

School Year: 1 2 3 4 5 6 7 8 9 10 11 12 13 14 15 16 17 18

Typical Age: 3 4 5 6 7 8 9 10 11 12 13 14 15 16 17 18 19 20 21 22 23 24

School subjects

The following table shows the subjects in Japanese schools under the new curriculum (introduced in 2002–3). Compare the subjects taught in a Japanese school with those taught in your school.

しょうがっこう 小 学 校		ちゅうがっこう 中 学 校		こうとうがっこう 高 等 学 校	
こくご	National Language (Japanese)	こくご	National Language (Japanese)	こくご	National Language (Japanese)
				• こてん	Classics
				• かんぶん	Chinese Literature
				• こぶん	Ancient Literature
しゃかい	Social Studies	しゃかい	Social Studies	ちり	Geography
				せかいし	World History
				にほんし	Japanese History
				こうみん	Civics
さんすう	Arithmetic	すうがく	Mathematics	すうがく	Mathematics
りか	Science	りか	Science	りか	Science
せいかつ	Life skills	• だい1 ぶんや	Science 1 (Chemistry and Physics)	• かがく	Chemistry
		• だい2 ぶんや	Science 2 (Physical Geography and Biology)	• せいぶつ	Biology
				• ぶつり	Physics
				• ちがく	Earth Science
				• じょうほう	Computing
おんがく	Music	おんがく	Music	げいじゅつ	Arts
ずこう	Drawing and Handicraft	びじゅつ	Art	• おんがく	Music
				• びじゅつ	Art
				• しょどう	Calligraphy
				• こうげい	Handcraft
かていか	Home Economics	ぎじゅつ かてい	Industrial Arts and Homemaking	かていか	Home Economics
		がいこくご	Foreign Language	がいこくご	Foreign Language
		• えいご	English	• えいご	English
		• ドイツご	German	• ドイツご	German
		• フランスご	French	• フランスご	French
たいいく	Physical Education	ほけん たいいく	Health and Physical Education	ほけん	Health
				たいいく	Physical Education
どうとく	Moral Education	どうとく	Moral Education		

Other subjects

1	えんげき	Speech and Drama	5	コンピュータ	Computing
2	しょうぎょうぼき	Commerce, Business Principles	6	しゅうきょう	Religion
3	ぎじゅつ	Manual Arts	7	れきし	History
4	ほうりつ	Legal Studies			

Once you have learnt the words for the subjects that you are studying, you are ready to use them in sentences.

You can already say that you play a particular sport:

やきゅうを　します。　　　　　　I play baseball.

You can tell someone what you are learning:

にほんごを　ならっています。　I am learning Japanese.

Using the same pattern but with different verbs, you can give information about what you are studying (べんきょうしています).

Note that べんきょうしています and ならっています imply that the activity of studying or learning is occurring now. On the other hand, します is more general and can also be used to imply a future activity. For example テニスを　します means 'I play tennis,' but it can also mean 'I will play tennis (later).'

覚えましょう
おぼ

Sentence pattern

Q しゃかいを
べんきょうしていますか。

Are you studying Social Studies/
Do you study Social Studies?

A はい、しゃかいを
べんきょうしています。

Yes, I am studying Social Studies/
Yes, I study Social Studies.

A いいえ、しゃかいを
べんきょうしていません。

No, I am not studying Social Studies.

Explanation

Notice how easy it is to change a sentence from the positive to the negative form: 'I am studying' to 'I am not studying'. As explained in sentence pattern 10, simply change the final す to せん.

べんきょうしています　　　I am studying
べんきょうしていません　　I am not studying

If someone asks what subjects you study, you may choose to list them all—in which case you would separate them with と, meaning 'and'. If, however, you want to name just a few but not the whole lot, you would separate them with や to mean '… and others'.

覚えましょう
おぼ

Sentence pattern

12

Q なにを　べんきょうしていますか。　What are you studying?

A えいごや　すうがくや
りかを　べんきょうしています。

I am studying English and Maths
and Science (and others).

A えいごと　にほんごと　りかと
すうがくと　しゃかいと
たいいくを　べんきょうしています。

I am studying English and Japanese
and Science and Maths and Social
Studies and Physical Education.

F   Education in Japan

日本について

Structure

- Kindergarten – one to three years.
- Primary or elementary school – six years.
- Junior high school (lower secondary) – three years; (95.8% progress to senior high school).
- Senior high school (upper secondary) – three years; (45.2% progress to higher education).
- University (usually four years), or college (usually two years).

日本について

School holidays and hours

- School year starts 1 April.
- School year ends 31 March the following year.
- Summer vacation: six weeks in July and August.
- Winter vacation: around New Year's holiday.
- Spring vacation: two to three weeks after annual exams.
- Lessons generally start at 8.30 am and finish at 3.00 pm.

日本について

Cram schools

Students sit for entrance exams to get into any school, and this causes great pressure and stress.

Because of the importance of getting into the best possible school, students may attend じゅく or cram schools. These offer private tutoring to help students prepare for exams.

The final year of senior high school is often referred to as じゅけんじごく ('exam hell').

日本について

Uniforms

School uniforms are compulsory in most junior and senior high schools. Whether there is a uniform or not depends on the particular education authority.

日本について
Clubs

Almost all junior high school and many senior high school students enrol in club activities at school. These occur after lessons for two to four hours. Typical club activities include: English conversation, history, acting, newspaper publication, chemistry, biology, tea ceremony, athletics, soccer, baseball, track and field, martial arts and swimming.

日本について
Class sizes

Because of Japan's ageing population and lower birth rate, class sizes have reduced to about 40 students per class. In 1990, the average class size was about 47.

日本について
School events

* にゅうがくしき (entrance ceremonies) in April.
* うんどうかい (athletics competitions) in September and October.
* ぶんかさい (cultural festivals) in September and October.
* そつぎょうしき (graduation ceremonies) in March.

日本について
School lunch

In many elementary schools and in some junior high schools, children eat lunch together in the classroom. School lunches, called きゅうしょく, are cooked on the school premises. They provide a well-balanced meal for young children.

In senior high schools, huge dining halls are common and students may buy a meal chosen from the menu.

日本について
Other

* The literacy rate in Japan is 99.7%
* Lessons begin and end with students bowing to teachers.
* Students are responsible for cleaning the school buildings and grounds.
* Students in junior and senior high school go away for up to a week on an excursion with their teachers. This excursion is called しゅうがくりょこう. Students commonly visit historical sites in Japan, such as the Toshogu Shrine in Nikko, or go skiing.

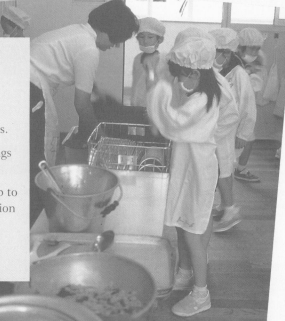

Favourite subjects

Andrew and Mariana have favourite subjects, just like their Japanese friends.

覚えましょう
_{おぼ}

Sentence pattern

13

Q いちばんすきな　かもくは
なんですか。

What is your favourite subject?

A （いちばんすきな　かもくは）
すうがくです。

(My favourite subject) is Maths.
/It is Maths.

Explanation

いちばんすきな　かもく is said as one phrase. However, it consists of three words:

いちばん Number one	+	すきな liked	+	かもく subject

Likes and dislikes

The following pattern is very useful when describing what subjects you like and dislike. In fact, it can be used when describing **anything** that you like or dislike.

覚えましょう
_{おぼ}

Sentence pattern

14

Q りかが　すきですか。　　　　　Do you like Science?

A はい、すきです。　　　　　　　Yes, I like it.

A いいえ、すきじゃないです。　　No, I don't like it.

A いいえ、りかは　すきじゃないです。　No, I don't like Science.

Explanation

Meaning marker が is similar in usage to は in that it, too, is a sign that points backward to the subject of the sentence. At this stage, just remember that you use が when you are saying that you like something. If you say you don't like something, use は.

日本語について

All very old documents in Japan were written vertically. However, with the introduction of modern pens (rather than brushes), arabic numerals, mathematical formulae and foreign 'alphabetic' words, the horizontal style is now used in many books. Most school texts (except Japanese Language and Classical Literature) are set in horizontal text. The horizontal form is very useful for texts on Science, Maths and other technical subjects. Most books and newspapers for a general readership (such as popular novels) are written in vertical text.

Sending emails

Mariana is trying to get to know Yoko, her soon-to-be host sister. So she sends her an email, to which Yoko replies immediately.

Read Mariana's email and Yoko's reply. What do the two girls have in common and what are their differences? (Mariana uses some new words. You should be able to work them out from the context and from what you know already.)

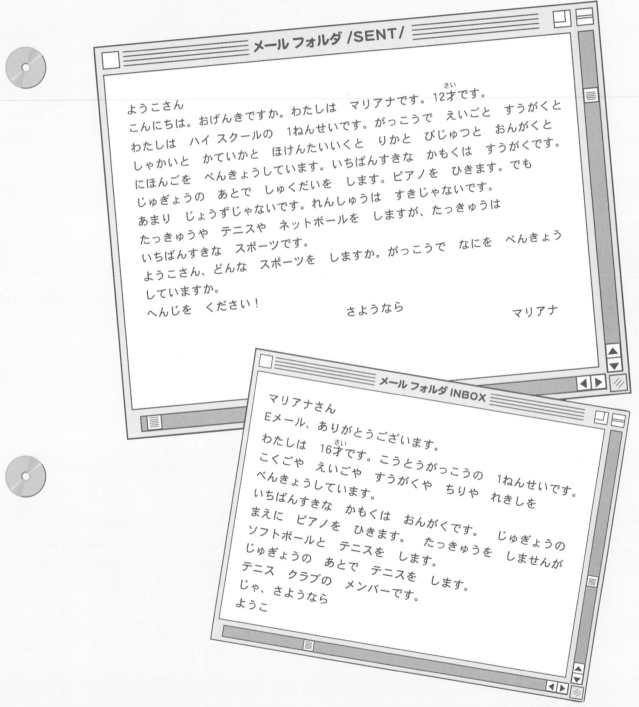

メールフォルダ /SENT/

ようこさん
こんにちは。おげんきですか。わたしは マリアナです。12才です。
わたしは ハイ スクールの 1ねんせいです。がっこうで えいごと すうがくと
しゃかいと かていかと ほけんたいいくと りかと びじゅつと おんがくと
にほんごを べんきょうしています。いちばんすきな かもくは すうがくです。
じゅぎょうの あとで しゅくだいを します。ピアノを ひきます。でも
あまり じょうずじゃないです。れんしゅうは すきじゃないです。
たっきゅうや テニスや ネットボールを しますが、たっきゅうは
いちばんすきな スポーツです。
ようこさん、どんな スポーツを しますか。がっこうで なにを べんきょう
していますか。
へんじを ください！

さようなら   マリアナ

メールフォルダ INBOX

マリアナさん
Eメール、ありがとうございます。
わたしは 16才です。こうとうがっこうの 1ねんせいです。
こくごや えいごや すうがくや ちりや れきしを
べんきょうしています。
いちばんすきな かもくは おんがくです。じゅぎょうの
まえに ピアノを ひきます。たっきゅうを しません
ソフトボールと テニスを します。
じゅぎょうの あとで テニスを します。
テニス クラブの メンバーです。
じゃ、さようなら
ようこ

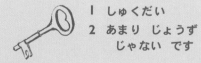

1	しゅくだい	homework	3 れんしゅう	practice
2	あまり じょうず じゃない です	I'm not very good at it		

セルフ　テスト

1　なにを　べんきょうしていますか。

2　ドイツごを　ならっていますか。

3　いちばんすきな　かもくは　なんですか。

4　にほんごが　すきですか。

5　しゃかいが　すきですか。

6　いちばんすきな　かもくは　りかですか。

7　Can you say the following words and phrases in Japanese instantly
… or do you have to think for a while?

- before school

- my favourite sport

- of course

- homework

- I'm not very good at it.

8　じゅぎょうのあとで　なにを　しますか。

9　がっこうで　コンピュータを　ならっていますか。

10　かていかを　ならっていませんか。

11　じゅぎょうの　まえに　ギターを　ひきますか。

12　いちばんすきな　スポーツは　バレーボールですか。

覚え方 (おぼ かた)　　Now is a good time to go back and redo the self-tests in Units 1–3.

5 かぞく
Families

Outcomes

By the end of this unit, you should be able to:
- explain how many people there are in your family and name them
- say where they work and what their occupations are
- explain what pets you have
- write an introductory letter to a Japanese pen-pal.

A₁ アンドルーさんの会話

Andrew has invited Toshio, a Japanese student visiting his school, to his home. With Andrew's Japanese, they are able to discover much about each other. Toshio is amazed at something else too. What is it?

1	ごかぞくは なん人ですか。	How many are there in your family?	
2	（ご）かぞく	(your) family	
3	五人	five people	
4	おばあさん	grandmother	
5	いもうと	younger sister	
6	いぬ	dog	
7	ペットを かっていますか	Do you keep any pets?	
8	おとうさんの	father's	

9	（ご）しょくぎょう	(your) job, occupation
10	コンピュータの プログラマー	computer programmer
11	きょうし	teacher
12	ぼくの おとうさん	my father
13	いしゃ	doctor
14	ただいま	I'm home!
15	おかえりなさい。	(Ah!) You've returned.
16	しんじられない。	I can't believe it!

A2　マリアナさんの会話

Mariana, too, is now able to have quite an extended conversation in her home with her Japanese friend Yuriko.

1	おにいさん	older brother	5	かんごふ	nurse
2	ペットを かっていません。	I don't keep any pets.	6	がっこうで	at (a) school
3	かいしゃいん	company employee	7	はたらいています	I/You work; I am/You are working
4	セールスマン	salesman	8	ほけんしつ	health room (sick bay at school)

Unit 5　**79**

Family names

You will later learn when to use particular words for family members, depending on whether they're your own relatives or someone else's. For now, the following terms will be sufficient. Remember to add さん to おとうと and いもうと if you are referring to the younger brother or sister of someone else.

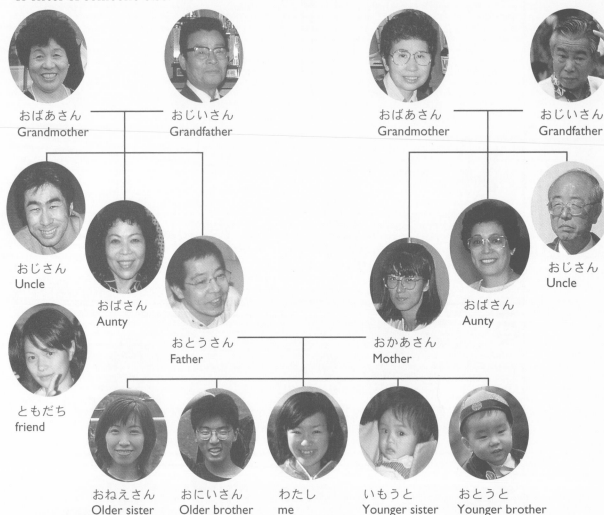

おばあさん
Grandmother

おじいさん
Grandfather

おばあさん
Grandmother

おじいさん
Grandfather

おじさん
Uncle

おばさん
Aunty

おとうさん
Father

おかあさん
Mother

おばさん
Aunty

おじさん
Uncle

ともだち
friend

おねえさん
Older sister

おにいさん
Older brother

わたし
me

いもうと
Younger sister

おとうと
Younger brother

日本について

Family life

The life expectancies of the Japanese are among the highest in the world, at 76.25 years for males and 82.51 years for females.

The average number of people per household is only 3.63, with fewer families now having more than one child.

While many families still include grandparents within the household (this has traditionally been the responsibility of the eldest son), this is becoming less common.

1	おじいさん	Grandfather	5	おねえさん	Older sister
2	おじさん	Uncle	6	いもうと（さん）	(your) Younger sister
3	おばさん	Aunty	7	おとうと（さん）	(your) Younger brother
4	ともだち	friend			

C1

覚えましょう
How many in your family?

Sentence pattern

15a

Q ごかぞくは　なん人_{にん}ですか。

How many people are there in your family?

A1 （かぞくは）五人_{ごにん}です。

There are five people in my family.

A2 （かぞくは）おとうさんと おかあさんと おにいさんと いもうとと　わたしです。

My family consists of my father, my mother, my older brother, my younger sister and me.

15b

Q なん人_{にん}　かぞくですか。

How many people are there in your family?

A 四人_{よにん}　かぞくです。

Four. (Literally: It is a four-person family.)

Explanation

For variety, you may choose to use the extension pattern 15b. Use ごかぞく when referring to someone else's family.

C2

Counting people

Look at the chart below. Remember how you add 才_{さい} to the basic numbers to count ages? To count people you add the kanji 人 to the numbers. This is usually read as にん as a counter for people, or as じん (as in にほんじん) when giving a nationality. Note that 'one person' and 'two people' are pronounced quite differently than all the rest, which follow an easy pattern. Check page 35 for the correct stroke order for 人.

1	一人	ひとり	6	六人	ろくにん
2	二人	ふたり	7	七人	しちにん／ななにん
3	三人	さんにん	8	八人	はちにん
4	四人	よにん	9	九人	くにん／きゅうにん
5	五人	ごにん	10	十人	じゅうにん

C3

An easy way to remember how to count people is to practise singing this song to the tune of 'Ten Little Indians':

ひとり　ふたり　さん人_{にん}　きました。 *One, two, three came.*
よ人_{にん} ご人_{にん} ろく人_{にん}　きました。 *Four, five, six came.*
しち人_{にん} はち人_{にん} きゅう人_{にん} きました。 *Seven, eight, nine came.*
じゅう人_{にん}の　いい　せいと。 *Ten good students.*

じゅう人_{にん}、きゅう人_{にん}、はち人_{にん}　でました。 *Ten, nine, eight left.*
しち人_{にん}、ろく人_{にん} ご人_{にん}　でました。 *Seven, six, five left.*
よ人_{にん} さん人_{にん} ふたり　でました。 *Four, three, two left.*
ひとりの　いい　せいと。 *One good student.*

覚えましょう
Occupations

Sentence pattern

16

Q おとうさんの　ごしょくぎょうは　なんですか。　What is your father's occupation?

A おとうさんは　けんちくかです。　My father is an architect.

Explanation

の is another meaning marker, as explained on page 52. It indicates that whatever comes before it owns the thing that comes after it. It has a similar function to **…'s** in English.

| Owner + の | + | the thing owned |

D2

8

9

10

What occupations could the people below possibly be engaged in?

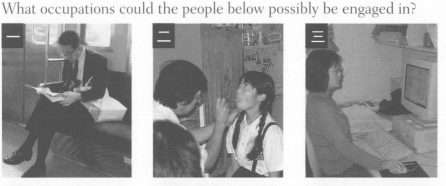

しょくぎょう (Occupations)

1	けんちくか	architect
2	きちょう	captain, pilot
3	だいく	carpenter
4	かいしゃいん	company employee
5	コンピュータの　プログラマー	computer programmer
6	はいしゃ	dentist
7	いしゃ	doctor
8	じゆうぎょうしゃ	freelancer (writer, photographer)
9	べんごし	lawyer
10	ぐんじん	member of armed forces
11	かんごふ	nurse

12	セールスマン	salesman
13	セールスウーマン	saleswoman
14	ひしょ	secretary
15	じえいぎょうしゃ	self-employed person
16	てんいん	shop assistant
17	がくせい	student
18	きょうし	teacher
19	むしょく	unemployed
20	ウェイトレス	waitress

E の can be used to help explain lots of things. What information do you know about each of these people?

2 わたしの かぞくは
五人です。

1 おかあさんの しょくぎょうは
かんごふです。

4 おにいさんの 一ばんすきな
かもくは すうがくです。

3 わたしの 一ばんすきな
かもくは にほんごです。

6 おとうとの 一ばんすきな
スポーツは からてです。

5 ぼくの なまえは アンドルーです。

日本について

A relatively new and growing phenomenon in Japan is loss of employment through company restructuring or even sacking. To explain this predicament to an acquaintance, you would say リストラされました ('ristora' is an abbreviation for 'restructure' of a company). Upon hearing this, the listener could say おきのどくですね。('That's really terrible, isn't it.')

7 おとうさんの しょくぎょうは
  かいしゃいんです。

F
11
12

覚えましょう
Places of work

Sentence pattern

17

Q おとうさんは どこで
   はたらいていますか。

Where does your Dad work?

A おとうさんは かいしゃで
   はたらいています。

Dad works/is working in a company.

Explanation

で is a meaning marker. It marks the place where an action takes place. Sometimes in English we use 'at' or 'in' for the same purpose.

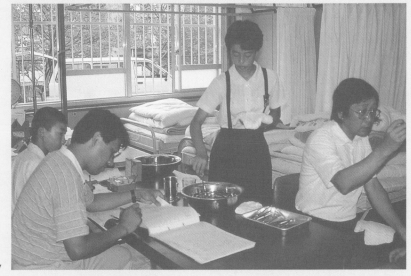

A junior high school sick bay

Other places where people work

1	みせで	at a shop		7	じむしょで	in an office
2	がっこうで	at a school		8	かいしゃで	in a company
3	ぎんこうで	at a bank		9	びょういんで	in a hospital
4	こうじょうで	at a factory		10	きっさてんで	in a coffee shop
5	デパートで	at a department store		11	ほけんしっで	in a sick bay (health room)
6	オフィスで	in an office		12	うちで	at home

覚えましょう
Family pets

Sentence pattern

18

Q	ペットを　かっていますか。	Do you have/keep a pet?
A	はい、いぬを　一匹 かっています。	Yes, I have a/one dog.
A	はい、ペットを　かっています。	Yes, I have/keep a pet.
A	はい、ペットを　二匹 かっています。	Yes, I have/keep two pets.
A	いいえ、ペットを　かっていません。	No, I don't have a pet.

Q　ペットを　かっていますか。
A　はい、いぬを　一匹（いっぴき）かっています。
A　はい、ペットを　かっています。
A　はい、ペットを　二匹（にひき）かっています。
A　いいえ、ペットを　かっていません。

Explanation

1 When counting small animals such as cats and dogs, another counter is used. You can see that the kanji for the number stays the same, as it does when you count people, but the pronunciation varies depending on how many you are counting.
When the two parts join together, sometimes the sound changes.

Counting small animals

1	一匹	いっぴき	4	四匹	よんひき
2	二匹	にひき	5	五匹	ごひき
3	三匹	さんびき			

One animal	=	一 いち	+	匹 ひき	=	一 いっ	匹 ぴき

2 If you want to make your sentence negative (that is, say that you don't have pets), remember that you simply change かっています to かっていません.

書きましょう^か

⑬ counter for small animals

かきかた (stroke order)

なりたち (history/origin)

Small animals rested their legs inside a kennel. As this pictogram was applicable to various animals, it was used as the counter for small animals. The pronunciation is ひき (or ぴき or びき depending on the number being counted).

おん　　ひつ
くん　　ひき
れい　　一匹　one animal
　　　　二匹　two animals

どうぶつ (Animals)

Which pets do you own? Of course, animals in Japan speak Japanese!

どうぶつ Animal(s)

1	いぬ	dog	6	うま	horse
2	モルモット	guinea pig	7	きんぎょ	goldfish
3	にわとり	chicken	8	ねずみ	mouse
4	あひる	duck	9	ねこ	cat
5	とり	bird	10	ひつじ	sheep

覚えましょう
What is it called?

Sentence pattern

19

Q　ねこの　なまえは　なんですか。　　　What is your cat's name?

A　「くろ」です。　　　　　　　　　　　It is 'Kuro'.

Explanation

You have already seen の at work in Unit 2 and sentence pattern 16 in this unit.

For example:

おとうさんの　ごしょくぎょう　　　　　Your father's occupation

わたしの　一ばんすきな　かもくは　りかです。　My favourite subject is Science.

ようこさんの　でんわばんごうは　なんばんですか。　What is Yoko's telephone number?

わたしの　でんわばんごうは　02の　5964の　2238です。　My telephone number is 02 5964 2238.

Remember that here の is like **...'s** so it denotes ownership.

I

19

What do these people have to say about their pets?

1　ペットを　二匹<ruby>二匹<rt>にひき</rt></ruby>　かっています。いぬと
ねこを　かっています。ねこの　なまえは
「カッドルズ」です。いぬの　なまえは
「ラッシー」です。

2　いぬの　なまえは「ともだち」です。
ねこの　なまえは「おに」です。
きんぎょの　なまえは「グッピー」
です。

3　ペットを　三匹<ruby>三匹<rt>さんびき</rt></ruby>　かっています。いぬと
モルモットと　とりを　かっています。
いぬの　なまえは「しろ」です。
モルモットの　なまえは「ふとっちょ」
です。とりは　カナリアです。なまえは
「ツイーティー」です。

1	...の　なまえ	...'s name	4	しろ	white ('Whitey')
2	くろ	black ('Blacky')	5	ふとっちょ	'fatty', blimp-like
3	おに	devil	6	カナリア	canary

Useful expressions

The following expressions are used daily whenever anyone leaves the house or comes home.

Before going out:

I'm going (and I'll come back).
See you later/Goodbye. ('Go and please come back.')

On coming home:

I'm home.
Welcome home. (You've returned.)

K

Putting it all together

When Andrew's new pen-pal writes to him, Andrew can understand quite a lot. See how much you can understand and then write a reply, ensuring that you answer all of Keiji's questions. Can you work out what the end of Keiji's letter is about?

アンドルーくんへ

　こんにちは。おげんきですか。ぼくは　おおさかに　すんでいます。ちゅうがっこうの　2ねんせいです。13才です。アンドルーくんは　なんねんせいですか。ぼくは　がっこうで　こくごと　えいごと　すうがくと　しゃかいと　おんがくと　りかと　どうとくを　べんきょうしています。アンドルーくんは　どうとくを　べんきょうしていますか。ぼくは　びじゅつを　べんきょうしていません。でも、ぎじゅつを　べんきょうしています。ギターを　ひきます。じゅぎょうの　あとで　ひきます。

　おとうさんは　48才です。けんちくかです。けんちくじむしょで　はたらいています。おかあさんは　45才です。かんごふです。しょうがっこうで　はたらいています。アンドルーくんの　おとうさんと　おかあさんの　ごしょくぎょうは　なんですか。

　ごかぞくは　なん人ですか。ぼくの　かぞくは　4人です。おとうさんと　おかあさんと　おとうとと　ぼくです。おとうとは　しょうがっこうの　3ねんせいです。

　アンドルーくんは　ペットを　かっていますか。ぼくは　ねこを　2匹　かっています。ねこの　なまえは　「こわい」と　「かわいい」です。

じゃ、へんじを　ください。

　　　　　　　さようなら

　　　　　　　　　　　　　　けいじより

追伸

「こわい」は　えいごで「scary」です。
「かわいい」は　えいごで「cute」です。
「けんちくじむしょ」は　えいごで　「architect's office」です。

Letter writing

Mariana received a letter from her Japanese friend Mai. Draw a picture of what you think Mai's family look like once they are ready for work in the morning. Label your sketch, providing as much information as you can about the family members.

Can you find and work out the meaning of the grammatical construction used in this letter but not yet introduced in this book?

こんにちは。
わたしは　ちゅうがっこうの　2ねんせいです。
13才です。
かぞくは　4人です。　おとうさん、おかあさん、
おねえさんと　わたしです。
おとうさんは　43才です。だいくです。
おかあさんは　42才で、かんごふです。おかあさんは　びょういんで
はたらいています。おねえさんは　てんいんです。　デパートで
はたらいています。
ペットを　2匹　かっています。いぬと　ねこを　かっています。
へんじを　ください。

さようなら

14年4月19日

せとぐち　まい

おとうさんは　だいくです。

ねこのなまえは　「しろ」です。

いぬのなまえは　「くろ」です。

1　ごかぞくは　なん人ですか。

2　おとうさんの　ごしょくぎょうは　なんですか。

or

おかあさんの　ごしょくぎょうは　なんですか。

3　おかあさんは　ひしょですか。

4　おとうさんは　どこで　はたらいていますか。

5　ペットを　かっていますか。

6　ごかぞくは　おとうさんと　おかあさんと　おねえさんと　おにいさんと
　　いもうとさんと　おとうとさんですか。

7　ともだちの　なまえは　なんですか。

8　What would you say in response to the following comments or questions?

　　a　いってきます。

　　b　ただいま。

　　c　おげんきですか。

9　なん人　かぞくですか。

10　ねこを　一匹　かっていますか。

覚え方　Have you been checking the vocabulary boxes regularly to see if you can remember all the words?

Andrew and Mariana are now ready for the next stage of their language-learning adventure — a couple of months in Japan. They will be living with Japanese families and going to school in Japan. You will continue your Japanese language-learning experiences with them. Let's go!

日本に　いきましょう

6 日本ゆき
Bound for Japan

Outcomes

By the end of this unit, you should be able to:
- explain what you will and will not eat and drink
- explain where you are going
- ask for particular food, drink and other things
- use a range of everyday expressions
- read simple menus
- discuss what you eat at particular meals
- use a variety of everyday expressions.

A₁ アンドルーさんの会話

Andrew and Mariana are now both ready to set off on the adventure of a lifetime — a holiday in Japan, staying with a host family.

みなさん、おはようございます。
わたしは　きちょうです。この度(たび)は
JALを　ごりよういただき、
まことに　ありがとうございます。
なお、おざせきの　ベルトを
おしめください。おねがいいたします。

すみませんが
わかりません！

らくに　して　ください。
だいじょうぶです。
The pilot is welcoming you aboard and is asking you to fasten your seat belt.

1 すみませんが	Excuse me, but …	3 らくに　して　ください。 Please relax.
2 わかりません。	I don't understand.	4 だいじょうぶです。 It's okay.

あとで・・・

1	あとで …	… after, later	5	… も	also
2	たべます	I/You eat	6	いきます	I/You go
3	わしょく	Japanese-style food	7	… に	to …
4	… ください	… please	8	わたしも	I too

A₂ マリアナさんの会話

Mariana, too, was able to engage in a simple dialogue with the flight attendant and was able to make herself understood.

あとで・・・

1	やすみ	holiday	4 おのみものは？	Would you like a drink?
2	がんばって！	Stick at it! Persist!	5 カルピスソーダ	Calpis soda
3	…べんきょうします	I/You (will) study …	6 …のみます	I/You (will) drink …

Unit 6　93

覚えましょう

Sentence pattern

20a

Q	なにを　たべますか。	What will/do you eat?
A	すしを　たべます。	I (will) eat sushi.

Sentence pattern

20b

Q	なにを　たべますか。	What will you eat?
A	すしを　ください。	Sushi, please.

Explanation

Whenever you want to ask for something, all you have to say is:

The thing that you want + を	+	verb-type ending ください。

Remember that を is a meaning marker. It indicates that whatever came before it is the object of the sentence.

Could I please have ...

When you are on a plane, you may find the following words useful. If you are asking for them, simply add …を　ください.

Food and drink

1	わしょく	Japanese-style food	7	ファンタ	Fanta
2	ようしょく	western-style food	8	コカコーラ	Coca-Cola
3	コーヒー	coffee	9	みず	water
4	こうちゃ	(black) tea	10	オレンジジュース	orange juice
5	りょくちゃ	green tea	11	ビール	beer
6	レモネード	lemonade	12	おちゃ	tea

Reading menus

Analyse the following menu and decide which meal you will order. As you can see, being able to read katakana is a great help in understanding a Japanese menu.

After you have decided what you will order, write a 'diary entry' in which you list what you will eat and drink during the meal about to be served. For example: りょくちゃを のみます。
I will drink green tea.

昼食（ちゅうしょく）
チキンカレーライス
又は（また）
ビーフストロガノフ
フェットチーネパスタ添え（ぞ）
フレッシュ サラダ
フレンチ ドレッシング
チョコレートアーモンドケーキ
ソフトロール ＆ バター
コーヒー 紅茶（こうちゃ） 緑茶（りょくちゃ）

ご到着前に（とうちゃくまえ）
ハムとチーズの
クロワッサン サンドウィッチ
マカデミアナッツ ビスケット
チョコレートバー
コーヒー 紅茶（こうちゃ） 緑茶（りょくちゃ）

1	又は	または	or	4	添え	…ぞえ	served with …
2	昼食	ちゅうしょく	lunch	5	紅茶	こうちゃ	black tea
3	ご到着まえに	ごとうちゃくまえに	prior to arrival	6	緑茶	りょくちゃ	green tea

C What?

なに means 'What?' When parents ask their children to do something, the children often respond by groaning な—に? 'Naaaani?'. To respond to a question with なに in it, just replace なに with the answer word, as you did when answering the question 'What are you studying?' on page 72 or 'What will you eat?' on page 94.

D More menus

You are on a plane for which the following menu is provided. List all the food items that you would eat or drink. Write each one in a separate sentence as shown in the example:

フレッシュ　サラダを　たべます。(I eat garden salad.)

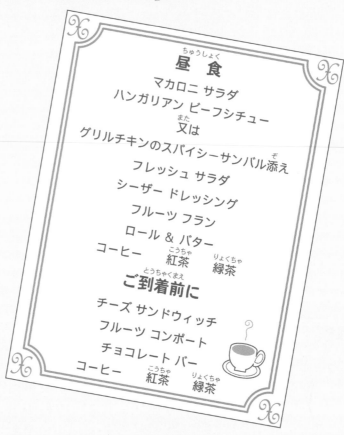

昼食（ちゅうしょく）

マカロニ サラダ
ハンガリアン ビーフシチュー
又（また）は
グリルチキンのスパイシーサンバル添（そ）え
フレッシュ サラダ
シーザー ドレッシング
フルーツ フラン
ロール ＆ バター
コーヒー　　紅茶（こうちゃ）　　緑茶（りょくちゃ）

ご到着前（とうちゃくまえ）に

チーズ サンドウィッチ
フルーツ コンポート
チョコレート バー
コーヒー　　紅茶（こうちゃ）　　緑茶（りょくちゃ）

E
6

There are undoubtedly some foods that you **don't** eat or drink. If you want to say that you **don't** eat or drink them, just change the 〜す at the end of a verb to 〜せん, as explained in sentence patterns 10, 11a and 11b.

覚えましょう
Meals

If you want to ask what someone eats for breakfast, for lunch or for dinner, all you have to do is add あさごはんに (for breakfast) or ひるごはんに (for lunch) or ばんごはんに (for dinner) to the beginning of your sentence, as shown in this sentence pattern.

Sentence pattern

21

Q あさごはんに　なにを　　　　What do/will you eat for breakfast?
たべますか。

A トーストを　たべます。　　　I (will) eat toast.

F2

Andrew meets a Japanese student on the plane and they discuss meals in their countries. What do these young people like eating? What would you have been able to add to this discussion?

一
ひるごはんに
サンドウィッチと
バナナを　たべます。
コカコーラを　のみます。

二
ひるごはんに
コカコーラを
のみますか？
わたしは
オレンジジュースを
のみます。わたしは
ひるごはんに
おべんとうを　たべます。

三
あさごはんに
なにを　たべますか。

たまごごはんを
たべます。

四
わたしは　オーストラリアで
ばんごはんに　ステーキを
たべます。にほんで
なにを　たべますか。

五
いろいろ　たべます。
すしを　たべますか。

とろ
ふとまき
ひかりもの

六
うに
はい、すしを　たべます。
でも、うにを　たべません。
うに

1	あさごはん	breakfast	5 たまごごはん	rice with raw egg
2	ひるごはん	lunch	6 いろいろ	various
3	ばんごはん	dinner	7 すし	raw fish on a finger of vinegared rice
4	おべんとう	boxed lunch	8 うに	sea urchin

Typical meals

What we eat at meal times varies from country to country, and also from person to person. If you were preparing a profile for a television documentary on dietary habits across the globe, what could you say about the following people? (Their typical meals are illustrated and labelled.) Look up the meaning of any words you do not know.

1 Name: Hiroshi Takeda
Age: 81 years of age
Nationality: Japanese

あさごはん
たまごやき
つけもの
ごはん
のり
みそしる

2 Name: Naomi Honda
Age: 14 years of age
Occupation: School student
Nationality: Japanese

ひるごはん
おべんとう

3 Name: Kensuke Kai
Age: 45 years of age
Occupation: Company employee
Nationality: Japanese

ばんごはん
てんぷら
ソース

4 Name: Colin McKnight
Age: 15 years of age
Occupation: Student
Nationality: Australian

ばんごはん
ロースト

5 Name: Gina Carlotti
Age: 13 years of age
Occupation: Student
Nationality: New Zealander

あさごはん
シリアル
ミルク
トースト
ジュース
トマト
ハムエッグ

Making requests

There are many distinctive Japanese foods. Most of them are available in our restaurants, and most of the ingredients can be purchased at Asian supermarkets. Use the World Wide Web and other sources to find out about the more commonly eaten Japanese foods.

When you wish to order or ask for something, use sentence pattern 20b. If you wish to be polite, you may choose to start your sentence with すみませんが … (Excuse me, but …).

Mariana and Andrew heard quite a few passengers using this pattern. They also heard people express gratitude in a variety of ways.

—Excuse me, could I have some water, please?
—Thank you.

—Excuse me, could I have a blanket, please?
—Thank you. (I'm very sorry for having bothered you.)
—You're welcome.

—Excuse me, could I have a cup of coffee, please?
—Here you are.
—Thanks.

—Excuse me, could I have a pen, please?
—Thanks very much.

すみません means several things. It can mean 'Excuse me'. It can also mean 'Thank you', 'I'm sorry' or 'I'm sorry to have put you to any bother' (see example 2).

—Excuse me, could I have some lemonade, please?
—Thanks.

Other things you might need

1	トランプ	(playing) cards
2	ブランケット	blanket
3	ペン	pen
4	はがき	postcard

覚えましょう
Where are you going?

Travellers commonly ask other travellers where they are going.

Sentence pattern

22

Q どこへ　いきますか。　Where are you going?/Where will you go?

A にほんへ　いきます。　I am going to Japan./I will go to Japan.

| Place + へ or に | + | verb いきます。 | I am/You are going to (place). |

Explanation

どこ is a question word meaning 'where'. へ and に both mean 'to' so either can be used.
Note that when へ is used as a meaning marker it is pronounced 'e'.
If it is clear in your sentences that you are talking about yourself, there is no need to put
わたし at the beginning.

覚えましょう
What about you?

Sentence pattern

23

Q にほんへ　いきます。あなたは？　I'm going to Japan. What about you?

A わたしも（にほんへ　いきます）。　I'm going to Japan too.

Explanation

Meaning markers は and を can be replaced by も to mean 'also' or 'too'. Be careful!
も cannot be put at the beginning or end of sentences.

Because も (meaning 'also' or 'too') replaces the meaning markers を and は, it can be used in
many sentence patterns. Look at these situations where も is used. Can you think of other
sentence patterns where it could be used?

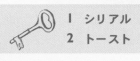

1	シリアル	cereal
2	トースト	toast

Useful expressions

I

12

If you want to reassure someone that you're okay, だいじょうぶ is a very useful expression that can be used in a wide range of situations.

—Oh! I'm sorry. Are you okay?
—Yes, I'm fine.

日本について

Tokyo is only one hour ahead of Eastern Standard Time in Australia and three hours ahead of New Zealand time. There is no problem with jet lag. Direct flights take about nine hours from Sydney to Tokyo.

The most common entry points into Japan are New Tokyo International Airport at Narita, near Tokyo, and Kansai International Airport near Osaka.

J

13

14

15

セルフ テスト

1 すしを たべますか。

2 にほんへ いきますか。

3 ともだちも がっこうに いきますか。

4 マリアナさんは ドイツに いきますか。

5 あさごはんに なにを のみますか。

6 ひるごはんに おべんとうを たべますか。

7 アンドルーさんは どこへ いきますか。

8 In what circumstances would you use these expressions?

   a どういたしまして。

   b だいじょうぶですか。

   c ええ、おかげさまで。

   d ごめんなさい。

   e すみませんが …

   f どうぞ。

   g ただいま。

9 あなたの いちばんすきな わしょくは てんぷらですか。

10 あなたの いちばんすきな ようしょくは パスタですか。

1	ごめんなさい	I'm sorry, excuse me
2	だいじょうぶ	safe, all right

わたしの ホストファミリー
My host family

A1

Andrew is being hosted by the Tanaka family in a traditional house in Osaka, so he has taken a connecting flight to Osaka to meet his 'host family'. Mariana will stay in Tokyo with the Ikeda family.

アンドルーさんの会話

一
アンドルーくん、
ようこそ。
わたしは たなか よしおです。
うちの かぞくです。

二
はじめまして、
どうぞ よろしく

こちらこそ。

三
おじいさんと おばあさんです。
けんすけと まりこです。
そして おかあさんです。

四
ホスト ファミリーに
なっていただいて、
ありがとうございます。

いいえ、
よろこんで！

1 わたしの ホストファミリー	my host family	5 ホスト ファミリーに なっていただいて … ... for becoming my host family
2 ようこそ。	Welcome.	
3 うちの かぞくです。	This is our family.	6 いいえ、よろこんで No, not at all. We are delighted (to be able to host you).
4 そして	and	

A₂ マリアナさんの会話

1	にほんへ ようこそ。	Welcome to Japan.	11 げんかん	entrance, front entry to a home
2	マンション	a unit, an apartment	12 にほんごは あまり わかりません。	I don't understand much Japanese.
3	… そとで	outside …	13 えいごで	in English
4	これ	this	14 … なかで	inside …
5	わたしたちの	our	15 どうぞゆっくり。	Please make yourself at home.
6	きれい	pretty	16 それ	that
7	ほら！	Hey!	17 すいはんき	rice cooker
8	みて！	Look!	18 すごい	cool, terrific
9	あれ	that over there		
10	はなび	fireworks		

覚えましょう
What is that?

Sentence pattern

24a

Q	これは　なんですか。	What is this?
A	これは　すしです。	This is sushi.

Sentence pattern

24b

Q	それは　なんですか。	What is that?
A	これは　すいはんきです。	This is a rice cooker.

Sentence pattern

24c

Q	あれは　なんですか。	What is that over there?
A	あれは　はなびです。	Those are fireworks (over there).

Explanation

1 In Unit 2 it was explained that は is a meaning marker, pointing to the topic of the sentence, i.e. the person or thing that you are speaking about. In Mariana's dialogues, the topic is this (これ) or that (それ) or that over there (あれ).

Mariana wants to ask about 'that thing there' so それ becomes the topic of the sentence. When her host mother gives her further information about the すいはんき, the rice cooker (すいはんき) becomes the topic, so it is followed by は. A simple way to translate は is 'as for …'.

2 In English we say 'this', 'that' and 'that over there', depending on the location of an object. So too do the Japanese.

- これ refers to something very close to the speaker.
- それ refers to something a little distance from the speaker but close to the listener.
- あれ is used to refer to something at a great distance from both speaker and listener.

3 In *Tsumiki 1*, これ, それ and あれ will always be used as the topic of a sentence, so they will nearly always be followed by は.

A typical feature of a Japanese home is a
ゆかしたの　ものいれ
('under-floor storage')

Finding out what's what

When you first arrive in Japan, there'll be many things whose names you won't know. Listen and observe as Andrew's 'host mother' takes him on a guided tour through the Japanese home.

While most newer homes in Japan today are not designed as they were fifty or sixty years ago, it is still common to have at least one わしつ (traditional Japanese-style room) in the house. Even in small マンション you can find interior features that are more typical of the traditional architecture. (For example, no matter the size or age of the dwelling, some sort of げんかん would be essential.)

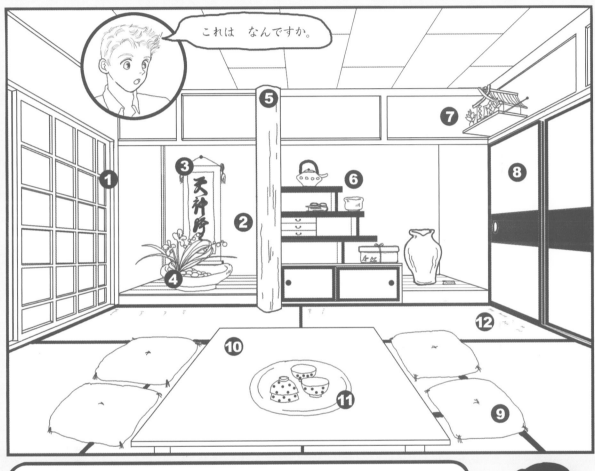

これは　わしつです。わしつは「traditional room」です。
1	これは　しょうじです。	7	これは　かみだなです。
2	これは　とこのまです。	8	これは　ふすまです。
3	これは　かけじくです。	9	これは　ざぶとんです。
4	これは　いけばなです。	10	これは　ざたくです。
5	これは　とこばしらです。	11	これは　ちゃわんです。
6	これは　ちがいだなです。	12	これは　たたみです。

1	しょうじ	paper screen (sliding door)	7	かみだな	household Shinto altar
2	とこのま	alcove in a traditional room	8	ふすま	sliding door inside home
3	かけじく	scroll hanging in a とこのま	9	ざぶとん	cushion for sitting on
4	いけばな	flower arrangement	10	ざたく	low table
5	とこばしら	wooden pole adjacent to とこのま	11	ちゃわん	tea cup / rice bowl
6	ちがいだな	staggered shelves	12	たたみ	rice-straw matting on floor

Other things you'll need to know when staying in a Japanese house …

1 それは「ものほしざお」です。

2 これは「ふとん」です。

3 これは「げんかん」です。

4 これは「トイレ」です。
これは「スリッパ」です。

(Notice the electronic controls that some modern Japanese toilets are fitted with.)

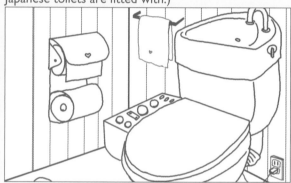

5 これは「エアコンの リモコン」です。
これは「テレビの リモコン」です。
これは「ビデオの リモコン」です。

6 これは「ふろば」です。

1	ものほしざお	clothes line (Japanese-style)	5	スリッパ	slippers
2	ふとん	quilts, bedding (traditional)	6	エアコンのリモコン	air conditioner remote control
3	げんかん	front entry to home	7	テレビのリモコン	television remote control
4	トイレ	toilet	8	ビデオのリモコン	video remote control
			9	ふろば	bathroom

C The pattern これは … です can be used in a variety of circumstances:

- to indicate what something is
- to 'introduce' your friend to your pet
  これは　うちの　いぬです।　　　This is the family dog.
- to point out people in a photograph.

However, it would be considered impolite to use it to directly introduce someone to another person. In this case, at this stage, it is best to clearly gesture to the person being introduced and say: ともだちです。ともこです।　　　This is a friend. This is Tomoko.

🗝 **1** うちの　いぬ　　　　family dog

覚えましょう
Whose is it?

Sentence pattern

25a

Q	だれのですか。	Whose is it?
A	わたしのです。	It is mine.
A	ゆみこさんのです。	It is Yumiko's.

Sentence pattern

25b

わたしの　ほんです。	It is my book.
わたしの　ほんじゃないです。	It is not my book.
わたしの　じゃないです。	It is not mine.

Explanation

1　の, when added to someone's name, shows that the person owns something. It is similar to **...'s** in English, as explained on page 87.

例	ゆみこさんのです。	It is Yumiko's.
	おかあさんのです。	It is Mother's.

2　In English, if we want to change 'I' to 'my' or 'mine' we have to change the whole word. Thus 'I own the book' becomes 'The book is mine' or 'This is my book'. Fortunately, this doesn't happen in Japanese. Just add a の to the person or thing that 'owns' something.

例	これは　ほんです。	This is a book.
	これは　わたしの　ほんです。	This is my book.
	それは　あなたの　えんぴつです。	That is your pencil.

You can see in the sentence pattern that の shows ownership or possession. If there is a の between two nouns, then the second thing is 'owned by' or 'a part of' the first.

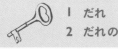

1	だれ	who	3　ほん	book
2	だれの	whose	4　えんぴつ	pencil

Who owns what around the house? It is always important, as a guest in someone's home, to know who has ownership over various things so that you don't upset the family routine. Mariana and Andrew soon work it out.

田中の　うち
たなか

池田の　うち
いけ だ

1	しんしつ	bedroom	4 せいふく	(school) uniform
2	いす	chair	5 タオル	towel
3	にわ	garden		

覚えましょう

Staying with a family who know at least some English can save you looking up everything in a dictionary.

Sentence pattern

26

Q 「さしみ」は えいごで なんですか。 What is sashimi in English?

A 「ローフィッシュ」です。 It is raw fish.

E₂ Mariana is eating lots of things that she has never seen before. Mr and Mrs Ikeda speak some English, so they are able to help her out when she's not sure whether or not she wants to eat something.

Can you answer Mariana's questions?

(The answers are illustrated on this page.)

さしみ

1 「さしみ」は えいごで なんですか。

2 「ちゃんこなべ」は えいごで なんですか。

3 「ラーメン」は えいごで なんですか。

4 「Stew」は にほんごで なんですか。

5 「Roast」は にほんごで なんですか。

6 「かまぼこ」は えいごで なんですか。

7 「ちゃわんむし」は えいごで なんですか。

8 「つけもの」は えいごで なんですか。

9 「みそしる」は えいごで なんですか。

10 「やきそば」は えいごで なんですか。

ちゃんこなべ

ラーメン

シチュー

かまぼこ

ちゃわんむし

おつけもの

ロースト

やきそば

みそしる

1	さしみ	sashimi, sliced raw fish	6	かまぼこ	steamed fish-paste cake
2	ちゃんこなべ	chanko nabe (stew for sumo wrestlers)	7	ちゃわんむし	savoury egg custard
			8	つけもの	pickles
3	ラーメン	Chinese noodles	9	みそしる	miso soup (made from fermented soy bean paste)
4	シチュー	stew			
5	ロースト	roast	10	やきそば	fried noodles like 'chow mein'

F

日本について

さしみ is sliced fish served raw: tuna, squid, prawn, mackerel and so on.

これは さしみです。

日本について

てっぱんやき is food (meat and vegetables) grilled on an iron or steel plate. The meal is cooked in front of you.

これは てっぱんやきです。

日本について

すし is a meal consisting of raw fish or egg on a finger of rice. Numerous varieties can be found outside Japan. These frequently make use of local ingredients such as avocado.

これは すしです。

日本について

みそしる is a soup made from fermented soy bean paste. It usually contains tofu and seaweed. It accompanies most Japanese meals.

これは みそしるです。

日本について

やきとり is chicken pieces skewered and cooked on a grill. A variety of chicken parts can be used — the chicken meat, liver or heart.

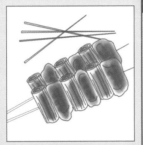

これは やきとりです。

日本について

ちゃわんむし is a steamed egg custard containing a mixture of certain meats, seafoods and vegetables.

これは ちゃわんむしです。

日本について

しゃぶしゃぶ is a meal of finely sliced beef, onion and other vegetables, cooked in boiling water in a pan in front of you. Once the meat and vegetables are cooked they can be dipped into a sauce.

これは しゃぶしゃぶです。

日本について

ごはん is boiled rice. Japanese people eat rice daily and sometimes with every meal. The fact that ごはん also means 'a meal' reflects the important role played by rice in the daily diet.

これは ごはんです。

日本について

おこのみやき is a kind of pancake made with eggs, flour and a selection of ingredients such as cabbage, other vegetables, pork, chicken or prawns. It is cooked at the table on a flat hotplate.

これは おこのみやきです。

日本について

つけもの are pickled vegetables. They are usually served as condiments to complement other dishes.

これは つけものです。

覚えましょう
Yes, it is … No, it isn't

Sentence pattern

27

Q	これは　すしですか。	Is this sushi?
A	はい、すしです。	Yes, it is sushi.
A	いいえ、（これは）すしじゃないです。	No, it is not sushi.

Explanation

To say that something is not something else, simply replace です with じゃないです.

G2

9

In this exercise, answer the question first by saying that it is not the food that you thought it to be, and then by saying what it is. In your exercise book, jot down some notes about the various foods.

Your teacher will be able to assist you with this exercise and you may be able to find out other information from Japanese cookbooks. Study the example carefully before you begin.

例

Q これは　おべんとうですか。
A いいえ、おべんとうじゃないです。すしです。

Sushi is raw seafood on a finger of rice. An obento is a boxed meal containing a variety of foods.

1　これは　コーヒーですか。

2　これは　たまごですか。

3　これは　にくですか。

4　これは　みそしるですか。

	1 たまご	egg		**2** にく	meat

H When you just don't understand

Just because your Japanese friend tells you the correct name for something, this doesn't mean that you really understand, so you might have to ask your friend to say it again. Because many Japanese can speak some English, they might be able to use some English words in their answer to make sure that you understand. Study this dialogue carefully.

You: すみませんが　これは　なんですか。

日本人: すきやきです。

You: すきやき… わかりません。にほんごは　あまり　わかりません。
(I don't understand much Japanese.)
すきやきは　えいごで　なんですか。

日本人: すきやきは「simmered vegetables and meat」です。

You: ああ、そうですか。ありがとう。
(Oh. Is that so. Thank you.)

With a partner, make up your own dialogue like the one above. Practise saying it until the expressions sound 'natural' and you can say them fluently.

I 覚えましょう

10

The Japanese are very proud of their cuisine and so will frequently ask you what you think of it. They are flattered if you try it, and delighted when you love it. The next sentence pattern allows you to pass compliments and make polite comments.

What's it like?

Sentence pattern

28

Q	それは　どうですか。	How is that?
Q	どうですか。	What's it like?
Q	いかがですか。	How is it?
A	おいしいです。	It's delicious.

Your Japanese host may be more specific and ask what you think of a particular food, as in this question:　すしは　どうですか。　　How is the sushi?

a You could answer with: すきです。I like it.

b It would be considered very rude to say that you don't like something, but you could say to your friends: まあまあです。 It's passable/okay.

c To your very good friends of your own age you could say: まずい（です）。It's awful.

d With food such as ようかん you might like to say: あまいです。It's sweet.

1	すきやき	vegetables and meat simmered in sauce	5 まあまあ	not bad, passable, okay
2	どうですか	How is it?	6 まずい	awful
3	いかがですか	How is it?	7 ようかん	sweet bean jelly
4	おいしい	delicious	8 あまい	sweet

Useful expressions

J

1 Before you eat anything offered to you or prepared by another, you say いただきます, which means 'I (humbly) receive (this delicious food)'.

2 When you have finished the meal you say ごちそうさまでした, meaning 'Thank you very much for the delicious meal and your kind hospitality'.

3 When you want to make someone feel welcome at your place, you say どうぞ　ごゆっくり, meaning 'Please make yourself at home'.

K

アンドルーさんの　しゃしん

A family photo album provides a good stimulus for conversation. With a little preparation, you will be able to initiate and sustain a conversation that your Japanese friend will be interested in.

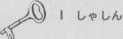

| 1 しゃしん | photo | 2 なんでも | anything |

L

Mariana prepared a photo album so that she could show her host family photos of her own family. Prepare a similar description of your own family.

これは　わたしの　かぞくの　しゃしんです。これは　おとうさんです。おとうさんは　クリスです。けんちくかです。けんちくじむしょで　はたらいています。これは　おかあさんです。モニークです。おかあさんは　かんごふです。びょういんで　はたらいています。これは　おにいさんです。ピーターは　こうこうせいです。17才です。これは　アンジェラです。アンジェラは　だいがくせいです。20歳です。これは　うちの　ねこです。ねこは　2才です。うちの　ねこは　ミルクを　のみません。みずを　のみます。

M

12

セルフ　テスト

1 これは　なんですか。

2 これは　すきやきですか。

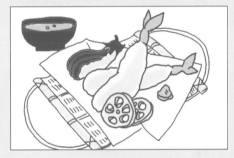

3 これは　アンドルーくんの　うちですか。

4 あれは　はなびですか。

5 それは　あなたの　がっこうですか。

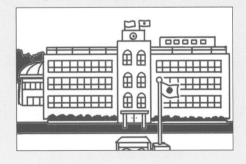

1	けんちくじむしょ	architect's office
2	こうこうせい	senior high school student
3	だいがくせい	university student
4	うちの　ねこ	family cat

8 たんじょうび
Birthdays

Outcomes

By the end of this unit you should be able to:
- wish someone a happy birthday
- provide information about your birthday
- express time using days, dates, months and general time words
- give someone's Chinese zodiac sign
- describe gifts.

A1 Andrew and Mariana both celebrate their birthdays while in Japan. Let's share in their celebrations and prepare for your own birthday.

アンドルーさんの会話

1	たんじょう日	birthday	5	おたんじょう日、おめでとうございます	Happy birthday
2	おたんじょう日	(someone else's) birthday	6	うれしい	(I'm so) happy/glad/rapt
3	アンドルーさんのおたんじょう日に	on Andrew's birthday	7	あけて	Open it up! (informal)
4	トントン	knock, knock	8	うさぎどし	Year of the Rabbit

マリアナさんの会話

一　六月三十日 (ろくがつさんじゅうにち)

マリアナさんの
おたんじょう日は　いつですか。

らいしゅうです。
七月七日です。(しちがつなのか)
土よう日です。(ど・び)
13才に　なります。(さい)

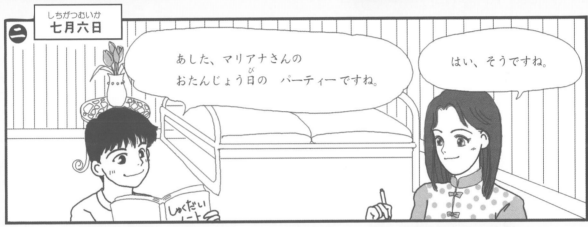

二　七月六日 (しちがつむいか)

あした、マリアナさんの
おたんじょう日の　パーティーですね。

はい、そうですね。

三　つぎの日 (ひ)（七月七日 (しちがつなのか)）7:00

ホームシックです。
きょうは　わたしの
たんじょう日です。

Sigh…

四

しずかに！
くるよ！

1	六月 三十日 (ろくがつ さんじゅうにち)	June 30	8　あした	tomorrow
2	いつ	when	9　ホームシック	homesick
3	らいしゅう	next week	10　きょう	today
4	七月七日 (しちがつなのか)	July 7	11　パーティー	party
5	なります	I/You (will) become	12　くるよ。	She is coming.
6	七月 六日 (しちがつ むいか)	July 6	13　…よ	(placed at the end of sentences to add emphasis)
7	つぎの日	next day		

1	わあー、びっくりした！	Wow, what a surprise!	**5** あけてください。	Please open it.
2	おめでとうございます	congratulations	**6** なんでしょうか。	I wonder what it is?
3	プレゼント	present, gift	**7** チョコレート	chocolate
4	どうぞ （あけてください）。	Go ahead please (open it).	**8** ちがう。	You're wrong/No, it isn't.

Birthday greetings

Sending birthday greetings to your Japanese friends is quite simple because there's no need to write much at all. Just learn these very easy expressions:

おたんじょうび　おめでとうございます or　おたんじょうび　おめでとう。

They simply mean 'Congratulations on your birthday' or 'Happy birthday'.

You'll sometimes see birthday cards written in kanji, looking like this:

お誕生日　おめでとうございます。

If you want to add an extra phrase in cards to your friends, meaning 'keep well' add げんきでね。If you wish to be very formal to your host parents or someone very senior to yourself, you may add another expression which means 'Take care of yourself!':

おからだを　たいせつに　してください。

Look at the following birthday cards and then design one that you could send to one of your Japanese friends.

For a young child

1才のおたんじょうび

はじめての
たんじょうび
おめでとう。

おめでとう！

For Mum or Dad

だいすきな　おかあさんへ

おたんじょうび
おめでとうございます。
おからだをたいせつに
してください。

A HAPPY BIRTHDAY

To a friend from lots of friends (e.g. classmates)

おたんじょうびにクラスのおともだち みんなから

おめでとう！

To a school friend

ハッピー♡バースデイ

13才のたんじょうび
おめでとう!!

C₁
覚えましょう
Birthdates
なん月ですか (What month is it?)

When sharing information about birthdays, the first thing you need to know is how to express the month in which it occurs.

Sentence pattern

29

Q おたんじょう日は　なん月ですか。 What month is your birthday?
A 七月です。 July.

いちがつ 一月 1月 January	に がつ 二月 2月 February	さんがつ 三月 3月 March	し がつ 四月 4月 April
ご がつ 五月 5月 May	ろくがつ 六月 6月 June	しちがつ 七月 7月 July	はちがつ 八月 8月 August
く がつ 九月 9月 September	じゅう がつ 十 月 10月 October	じゅう いちがつ 十 一月 11月 November	じゅうにがつ 十二月 12月 December

C₂
書きましょう

The kanji for month (月)(pronounced がつ、げつ or つき) and day (日)(ひ、び、にち or か) are particularly useful when reading a Japanese calendar. Both are pronounced in several ways, depending on their usage.

14 moon, month

なりたち (history/origin)

Clouds are floating past the *moon*.

かきかた (stroke order)

丿 冂 月 月

おん　　がつ、げつ
くん　　つき
れい　　月 moon, 一月 January,
　　　　月よう日 Monday

15 sun, day

なりたち

This kanji was originally a more graphic illustration of the sun.

かきかた

丨 冂 日 日

おん　　にち、じつ
くん　　ひ、び、か
れい　　日よう日 Sunday

1 なん月　　　　What month?

覚えましょう

なん日ですか (What day of the month?)

The next information to give when talking about birthdays is the day of the month.

How the day of the month is written

How the day of the month could be written on a calendar

How the day of the month is pronounced

しちがつ
7月

日	1 一日 ついたち	8 八日 ようか	15 十五日 じゅうごにち	22 二十二日 にじゅうににち	29 二十九日 にじゅうくにち
月	2 二日 ふつか	9 九日 ここのか	16 十六日 じゅうろくにち	23 二十三日 にじゅうさんにち	30 三十日 さんじゅうにち
火	3 三日 みっか	10 十日 とおか	17 十七日 じゅうしちにち	24 二十四日 にじゅうよっか	31 三十一日 さんじゅういちにち
水	4 四日 よっか	11 十一日 じゅういちにち	18 十八日 じゅうはちにち	25 二十五日 にじゅうごにち	
木	5 五日 いつか	12 十二日 じゅうににち	19 十九日 じゅうくにち	26 二十六日 にじゅうろくにち	
金	6 六日 むいか	13 十三日 じゅうさんにち	20 二十日 はつか	27 二十七日 にじゅうしちにち	
土	7 七日 なのか	14 十四日 じゅうよっか	21 二十一日 にじゅういちにち	28 二十八日 にじゅうはちにち	

Days of the week

On a calendar, Sunday to Saturday can be abbreviated to just the first kanji of the full word. Sunday means 'day of the sun', shown by the kanji 日. The kanji for Monday, 月, means 'moon', as you saw on the previous page.

日本語について

The first day of the month (ついたち) is irregular because it is derived from a word based on the lunar calendar. つきたち (月立) was a word meaning 'moon standing'. The position and shape of the moon were important to the rice farmers as they indicated a particular part of the rice growing cycle. The time when the moon was narrow and vertical marked the first day of each month.

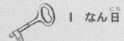

1 なん日   What day (of the month)?

書きましょう

In reading the Japanese calendar you would have seen the kanji for the days of the week. On page 121 you saw how to write the kanji for 'day' (used in each day of the week), and 'moon' (used in Monday). Now try writing the other days of the week so that you can answer appropriately when asked about the day your birthday is on.

例 なんよう日ですか。 What day (of the week) is it? 月よう日です。 It is Monday.

16 fire

かきかた (stroke order)

`、 ゛ ゾ 火`

おん　　か
くん　　ひ
れい　　火よう日 Tuesday

なりたち (history/origin)

 → 火

The crossed logs are burning brightly in the fire.

17 water, liquid

かきかた

`丨 刁 氺 水`

おん　　すい
くん　　みず
れい　　水 water
　　　　水よう日 Wednesday

なりたち

 → 水

The water is flowing down the river.

18 tree, wood, plant

かきかた

`一 十 才 木`

おん　　ぼく、もく
くん　　き
れい　　木よう日 Thursday

なりたち

 → 木

It is easy to see how this kanji represents a tree.

19 gold, money, metal

かきかた

`ノ 人 亼 今 仐 全 全 金`

おん　　きん、こん
くん　　かね
れい　　金よう日 Friday

なりたち

 → 金

Pitch a tent and dig for gold. It's not found in the two top layers but where the arrow is pointing.

20 soil, land, ground

かきかた

`一 十 土`

おん　　ど、と
くん　　つち
れい　　土よう日 Saturday

なりたち

→ 土

Plants grow up from the ground or earth.

🔑 1 なんよう日 What day (of the week)?

覚えましょう
だれの　おたんじょうび　ですか。(Whose birthday is it?)

Sentence pattern

30a

Q　おたんじょう日は　いつですか。　　When is your birthday?

Q　ようこさんの　おたんじょう日は　　When is Yoko's birthday?
　　いつですか。

A　（ようこさんの　おたんじょう日は）　(Yoko's birthday is) 10 July.
　　7月10日です。

Sentence pattern

30b

Q　だれの　おたんじょう日ですか。　　Whose birthday is it?

A　わたしの　たんじょう日です。　　It's my birthday.

Explanation

1　Because の is a meaning marker denoting ownership, it is used in the question 'Whose birthday is it?'

2　Note the use of お before たんじょうび when you are referring to someone else's birthday. It is a way of showing respect to others.

おたんじょう日は　いつですか。(When is your birthday?)

Write these people's birthdays in Japanese, using the pattern given. Write in the furigana as well as the kanji for the dates to practise how the date is said. Remember to reverse the order of names for these Japanese people.

例　(name) さんのおたんじょう日は　12月6日 です。

September 29

Sachiko Ueno

April 1

Tadahiro Nakano

May 5

Yoko Ishikawa

June 13

Ken Yamagata

March 6

Keiko Matsuda

January 20

Kyoko Kotani

August 8

Hanako Iwata

February 7

Yuki Suzuki

November 11

Takuya Yamamoto

December 2

Yoshiyuki Mifune

July 9

Akira Honda

October 3

Masa Hashida

覚えましょう

31

Q	マリアナさんは なにどしですか。	What is Mariana's Chinese zodiac sign?
A	マリアナさんは たつどしです。	Mariana was born in the Year of the Dragon.
	ようこさんは？	What about Yoko?

H₂

13

14

なにどしですか (What is your Chinese zodiac sign?)

In Japan it is said that your character and destiny are determined by the year in which you are born. In which year were you born?

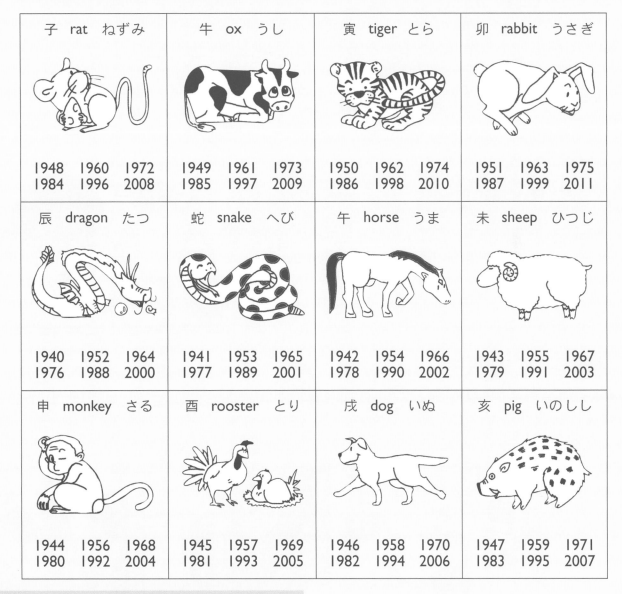

子 rat ねずみ
1948 1960 1972
1984 1996 2008

牛 ox うし
1949 1961 1973
1985 1997 2009

寅 tiger とら
1950 1962 1974
1986 1998 2010

卯 rabbit うさぎ
1951 1963 1975
1987 1999 2011

辰 dragon たつ
1940 1952 1964
1976 1988 2000

蛇 snake へび
1941 1953 1965
1977 1989 2001

午 horse うま
1942 1954 1966
1978 1990 2002

未 sheep ひつじ
1943 1955 1967
1979 1991 2003

申 monkey さる
1944 1956 1968
1980 1992 2004

酉 rooster とり
1945 1957 1969
1981 1993 2005

戌 dog いぬ
1946 1958 1970
1982 1994 2006

亥 pig いのしし
1947 1959 1971
1983 1995 2007

1 なにどし   What is your Chinese zodiac sign?

I Just wondering!

When opening presents, it is natural to wonder what the gift is.

Q	なんですか。	What is it? (Used amongst friends)
Q	ほんですか。	Is it a book?
A	いいえ。	No.
A	そうじゃないです。	It isn't.
A	はい、そうです。	Yes, it is.
Q	なんでしょうか。	I wonder what it is? (Formal, used by anyone)
Q	ほんでしょうか。	I wonder if it is a book?
A	ちがう。	You're wrong!/No it isn't. (Used amongst friends)
A	ちがいます。	You're wrong! (A more polite response)
A	おしい！	You're close. (What a shame. You just missed.)

J Useful expressions

15

After someone has given you a gift, you may use one of these expressions.

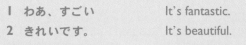

1	わあ、すごい	It's fantastic.
2	きれいです。	It's beautiful.
3	おもしろそうです。	It looks interesting.
4	すてき	It's great.
5	すごくいい！	It's excellent.

わあ、すごい！

When delicious-looking food is placed in front of you, try using: おいしそうですね。(This looks delicious!)

K₁ Please ...

By now Mariana and Andrew have become familiar with polite requests from others. They have quickly learnt that when they hear ください they've got to do something.

Can you work out what is being requested in each of these situations?

すわって ください。

しずかに して ください。

あけて ください。

K2

Your own classroom teacher will also use lots of these requests. Some others were introduced on page 40.

16

1	しゅくだいを して ください。	Please do your homework.
2	はなさないで ください。	Please don't talk.
3	れんしゅうして ください。	Please practise.
4	がんばって ください。	Stick at it.

L

In dialogue A2 of this unit, とし says:

あした、マリアナさんの おたんじょう日の パーティーですね。

17

あした is a general time word. When we talk about 'tomorrow' in English, we don't add any preposition like 'on' or 'at'. Neither do the Japanese. (When you wish to emphasise the time, は could be used, but don't worry about that now.)

In the next sentence pattern, see how 'time' words are placed at the beginning of a sentence.

覚えましょう
Time words

Sentence pattern

32

Q	あした パーティーを します か。	Are you having a party tomorrow?
A	はい、あした パーティーを します。	Yes, I am having a party tomorrow.
A	いいえ、あした パーティーを しません。	No, I'm not having a party tomorrow.

General time	+	object + を	+	verb

M

18

Here are some useful general time words and examples of how you can use them:

a あした　パーティーに　いきます。　　　　I'm going to a party **tomorrow**.

b きょう　がっこうに　いきます。　　　　　I'll go to school **today**.

c こんしゅう　がっこうに　いきません。　　I'm not going to school **this week**.

d らいしゅう　メルボルンに　いきません。　I'm not going to Melbourne **next week**.

e ことし　にほんごを　べんきょうします。　I'll study Japanese **this year**.

f らいねん　びじゅつを　べんきょうします。I'll study art **next year**.

g いま　にほんごを　べんきょうしています。I am studying Japanese **now**.

h ことし　フランスごを　ならっています。　I am learning French **this year**.

i らいねん　ドイツごを　ならいます。　　　I will learn German **next year**.

j あした　ピアノを　れんしゅうします。　　I will practise the piano **tomorrow**.

N

19

覚えましょう
なんよう日に　(On what day?)

When you want to be more specific about when things happen (for example, 'on Monday'),
you need to add the word 'on', as shown in this sentence pattern:

Sentence pattern

33

Q なんよう日に　パーティーを　　On what day are you having a party?
　　しますか。

A 土よう日に　パーティーを　　　I am having a party on Saturday.
　　します。

Day of the week + に	+	Object + を	+	verb
		(optional)		

日本について

Japanese department stores open
on Sunday. The streets are
sometimes closed to traffic (as in
the Ginza, Harajuku and
Akihabara) to create pedestrian
malls. These department stores
close on one other day during the
week (commonly on Tuesday).

日本について

Japanese schools have been
gradually reducing the
number of Saturdays when
students are required to
attend. There has been no
school on Saturday since
the beginning of 2002.

1	あした	tomorrow	6	らいねん	next year
2	きょう	today	7	いま	now
3	こんしゅう	this week	8	ならいます	I/you (will) learn
4	らいしゅう	next week	9	れんしゅうします	I/you (will) practise
5	ことし	this year			

覚えましょう
I'll turn 14 ...

Sometimes, when giving your age, it is better to say what you soon will be. For example, if your birthday is next week, and you will turn 14 years of age, you might find it strange saying that you are 13. The following pattern is useful to know in this context, and you will later learn how to use it in many other situations.

Sentence pattern

34

Q	なん才^{さい}ですか。	How old are you?
A	らいしゅう　14才に　なります。	I turn (become) 14 years of age next week.
A	月^{げつ}よう日^びに　14才に　なります。	I turn 14 years of age on Monday.
A	11月^{がつ}に　14才に　なります。	I turn 14 years of age in November.

Diary writing

Andrew and Mariana try to keep their diaries up to date. Knowing how to express time and the days of the week is extremely important for this. (Note that は can be used to emphasise the topic of the sentence. Therefore, in the asterisked sentences below, Mariana is emphasising that certain things will occur today.)

Umeda Sky Building

マリアナさんのジャーナル

8月23日
きょうは*　月よう日です。がっこうに　いきます。
きょう　すうがくを　べんきょうしません！すごい！
8月24日
きょうは*　火よう日です。　きょうは*　えいごの
せんせいの　おたんじょう日です。ひるごはんに
パーティーを　します。せんせいは　42才^{さい}です。
土よう日に　せんせいの　うちへ　いきます。

アンドルーさんのジャーナル

土／
らいしゅうの　月よう日に　こうべへ　いきます。
（おばあさんの　ともだちは　こうべに　すんで
います。）きょう　ひるごはんの　あとで、
うめだスカイビルに　いきます。そのあと、
でんでんタウンに　いきます。
日／
きょう、おはつてんじんへ　いきます。

1	うめだ　スカイビル	Umeda Sky Building
2	そのあと	after that
3	でんでんタウン	Electric City
4	おはつ　てんじん	Ohatsu Tenjin Shrine

The seasons in Japan are the opposite to those experienced in Australia and New Zealand.
Each season is quite distinct:
- **Winter** — December, January, February
- **Spring** — March, April, May
- **Summer** — June, July, August
- **Autumn** — September, October, November

From early June to mid July there is a humid rainy period. In late summer and autumn,
Japan is frequently struck by violent typhoons.

Q セルフ テスト

1 おたんじょう日は　いつですか。

2 きょうは　水よう日ですか。

3 なにどしですか。

4 らいねん　おたんじょう日の　パーティーを　しますか。

5 おたんじょう日は　なん月ですか。

6 おたんじょう日は　なん日ですか。

7 Match the expressions on the left with the times you would use those expressions
on the right.

a	すごくいい	When admiring the food your mother has put on the table.
b	きれいですね	When describing how fantastic/cool/terrific something is.
c	おかえりなさい	When exclaiming how happy you are.
d	おたんじょう日 おめでとう	When telling a friend that s/he is almost right.
e	ただいま	When your father returns home from work.
f	うれしい	When telling a friend that they are wrong.
g	ちがう	When you arrive home from school.
h	おいしそうですね	When wishing someone a happy birthday.
i	おしい	When saying how excellent something is.
j	すごい	When expressing how pretty something is.

8 ことし　なん才に　なりますか。

9 にっか
Daily routines

Outcomes

By the end of this unit, you should be able to:
- make simple descriptive observations
- describe your daily routine
- express an opinion about something
- express the time of day
- talk about periods of time in relation to your school timetable.

A₁ A day in the life of a teenager in Japan can be very busy. The following dialogue gives you an idea of what it can be like.

アンドルーさんの会話

一 アンドルーくん、がっこうは どうですか。

たのしいです。
せんせいが すきです。
クラスの みんなが すきです。
えいごが すきですが すうがくは まあまあです。

二 こくごは どうですか。

こくごは むずかしいですね。

三 うん、そうですね。

じゅくは すきじゃないです。

四 でも、アンドルーくんは じゅくへ いきませんね。

そうですが おにいさんは いきます。
よる ９じに うちに かえります。

1	たのしい	fun, enjoyable	
2	クラスの みんな	everyone in the class	
3	むずかしい	difficult	
4	うん	yes (informal)	

5	じゅく	cram school
6	よる	(in the) evening/(at) night
7	…じ	… o'clock
8	かえります	I/You (will) return

| 1 そうじ | cleaning (noun) | 3 クラブ | club |
| 2 たのしい | fun/enjoyable | 4 ちょっと | a bit |

Expressing opinions

Expressing your opinion about something or asking others for their opinion is an easy way of demonstrating that you wish to be fully engaged in dialogue—even though, as beginning Japanese students, you won't understand everything your Japanese friend says back to you. In Unit 7, sentence pattern 28, you learnt how to ask for someone's opinion about something:

（それは）どうですか。 　　　　　　　　How is that?/What is that like?

The same pattern could be used in the following way:

Q クラブは　どうですか。 　　　　What do you think about your club activity?
　　　　　　　　　　　　　　　　　　(Literally: 'As for club activity, how is it?')

A たのしいです、けど　ちょっと　　It's fun (I enjoy it) but it's a bit hard.
　　たいへんです。

You have already learnt some words that can be used to describe things. Here are a few more!

More describing words

1	たいへん	hard
2	たのしい	fun, enjoyable
3	おなじくらい	about the same
4	へん	strange, odd
5	おもしろい	interesting
6	いい	good
7	ハンサム	handsome

Remember these?

1	うつくしい	beautiful
2	かわいい	cute
3	まあまあ	not bad
4	おいしい	delicious
5	おいしそう	looks delicious
6	すき	(I) like
7	すきじゃない	(I) don't like
8	かっこいい	cool, attractive, trendy
9	じょうず	skilful
10	おなじ	same
11	すごい	fantastic, cool, terrific
12	きれい	pretty, beautiful
13	すごくいい	excellent, really good
14	おもしろい	interesting
15	おもしろそう	looks interesting
16	むずかしい	difficult
17	すてき	great, lovely

かっこいい

 1 けど 　　　　but, however (short form of けれども)

Describing things

There are many contexts within which you might like to use the describing words introduced on page 134. You could use them in response to the question … どうですか, or you could use them to generate conversation.

一　わあ、きれいですね。

二　すしが　すきです。

三　さしみが　すきじゃないです。

四　ラーメンは　どうですか。　ラーメンは　すきじゃないです。

五　にほんごは　おもしろいです。

六　パーティーは　たのしいです！

七　へんですね。

八　すうがくは　まあまあです。

九　かわいいですね！

十　ハンサムですね。

C 覚えましょう
Giving the time—the hour

Giving the time is a very easy language pattern, especially as you have already mastered the basic numbering system.

Sentence pattern

35

Q	いま なんじですか。	What time is it now?
A	いちじです。	It is one o'clock.

Number + じ + です。　　　It is … o'clock.

Explanation

Note that a particular form of the number is used when saying 4 o'clock, 7 o'clock and 9 o'clock.

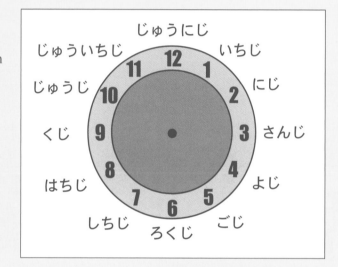

じゅうにじ
じゅういちじ　　いちじ
じゅうじ　　　　　　　にじ
くじ　　　　　　　　　さんじ
はちじ　　　　　　　　よじ
しちじ　ろくじ　ごじ

日本について

Japanese have a strong sense of group loyalty. The needs of the group are seen to be more important than those of individuals who belong to that group. Japanese feel very comfortable where order is maintained by giving priority to the group rather than to an individual. An important factor in maintaining order is keeping strictly to time.

Japanese tend to be precise about how long their walk to school takes and how long a train trip takes. Trains come and go with amazing punctuality. The 9.03 train always arrives at 9.03. Schools, too, are ordered places and punctuality is demanded.

| I | なんじ | What time? |

Busy train station

覚えましょう

Half past ...

When giving the half hour, simply put the word for 'half' after the hour.

Sentence pattern

36

Q	いま なんじ ですか。	What time is it (now)?
A	にじはんです。	It is half past two.

$\boxed{\text{Number}} + \boxed{じ} + \boxed{はん} + \boxed{です。}$ = It is half past …

Action!

You have already learnt some action words (verbs), and we know that they always go at the end of a Japanese sentence.

1	すしを たべます。	I **eat** sushi.
2	コーヒーを のみます。	I/We **drink** coffee.
3	えいごを べんきょうしています。	I **am studying** English.
4	らいねん フランスごを べんきょうします。	I **will study** French next year.
5	がっこうに いきます。	I/We **go** to school.
6	いぬを かっています。	I **have** a dog.

You can now add eight new verbs to your vocabulary. Sentence pattern 37 will show how these verbs can be used.

1	じゅぎょうは 9じに はじまります。	Lessons **start** at 9 o'clock.
2	じゅぎょうは 3じはんに おわります。	Lessons **finish** at 3.30.
3	6じに うちに かえります。	I **return** home at 6.00.
4	8じに がっこうに きます。	I **come to** school at 8 o'clock.
5	6じに おきます。	I **get up** at 6 o'clock.
6	10じはんに ねます。	I **go to bed** at 10.30.
7	8じはんに がっこうに つきます。	I (will) **arrive** at school at 8.30.
8	8じに うちを でます。	I (will) **leave** the house at 8 o'clock.

1	はじまります	(something) begins/will begin	5	おきます	I/You (will) get up (out of bed)
2	おわります	(something) ends/will end	6	ねます	I/You (will) go to bed (sleep)
3	かえります	I/You will return (home)	7	つきます	I/You (will) arrive
4	きます	I/You (will) come	8	でます	I/You (will) leave

覚えましょう
Doing things at particular times

Sentence pattern

37

a	**Q**	なんじに うちに かえりますか。	At what time will you return home?
	A	7じに かえります。	I'll return at 7 o'clock.
b	**Q**	1じかんめは なんじに はじまりますか。	At what time does Lesson 1 start? (Literally: 'As for Lesson 1, at what time does it start?')
	A	9じに はじまります。	It starts at 9 o'clock.
c	**Q**	パーティーは なんじに おわりますか。	At what time does the party finish?
	A	10じはんに おわります。	It will finish at 10.30.
d	**Q**	なんじに おきますか。	At what time do you/will you get up (out of bed)?
	A	6じはんに おきます。	I get up/will get up at 6.30.
e	**Q**	10じはんに ねますか。	Do you go to bed at 10.30?
	A	いいえ、10じはんに ねません。	No. I don't go to bed at 10.30.
	A	11じはんに ねます。	I go to bed at 11.30.
f	**Q**	いま がっこうに きますか。	Are you coming to school now?
	A	はい、いま いきます。	Yes. I'm going now.
g	**Q**	なんじに がっこうに つきますか。	At what time do you arrive at school?
	A	8じはんに つきます。	I arrive at 8.30.
h	**Q**	なんじに うちを でますか。	At what time do you leave the house?
	A	8じに うちを でます。	I leave the house at 8 o'clock.

日本について

Lessons in Japanese high schools are generally of 50 minutes duration and those in primary schools are usually 45 minutes long. There are five to six periods in a day (usually six in high school).

1 1じかんめ   lesson 1

G1 覚えましょう
From ... to ...

In the course of a day at school we go from one place to another. Lessons are from one time to another (for example, 9.00 to 10.00). The phrases 'from ... to ...' or 'from ... until ...' in the next sentence pattern are useful when describing your routine.

Sentence pattern

38

a 1じかんめは 9じから　　　　　　Period 1 is from 9.00 until 10.00.
10じまで　です。

b きょう　とうきょうから　　　　　　Today I'll go from Tokyo to Osaka.
おおさかまで　いきます。

c 7じから　9じはんまで　　　　　　I do homework from 7.00 to 9.30.
しゅくだいを　します。

Explanation
It is also possible to use から or まで without the other half of the phrase.

例 7じから　しゅくだいを　します。　　I do homework from 7.00.
きょう　おおさかまで　いきます。　　Today I'll go as far as Osaka.

G2 覚えましょう
Being specific about time

The following sentence patterns allow you to talk about the minutes before and after the hour, so that the listener knows exactly when you mean.

Sentence pattern

39

Q いま　なんじ ですか。　　　　　　What time is it (now)?
A 7じ5ふんです。　　　　　　　　　It is five past seven.

Sentence pattern

40

Q いま　なんじ ですか。　　　　　　What time is it (now)?
A 9じ10ぷんまえです。　　　　　　It is ten to nine.

Explanation
Note that the sound for 'minute', ふん, changes to ぷん when saying 1, 3, 4 and 6 minutes. Ten minutes is じゅっぷん.

1 ふん、ぷん　　minute
2 まえ　　　　　before (the hour)

H じかんわり (Timetables)

This timetable is typical for a Japanese junior high school student. How does it compare with yours? You may need to refer to page 71 to revise the names of the school subjects. Can you work out the meaning of the reminders on the sides?

中学校2年1組　時間わり　名前：_____

わすれものはないですか。

しゅくだいをしましたか

エンピツをけずりましたか。

		月	火	水	木	金
9.00	一時間目	国語	数学	国語	理科	国語
10.00	二時間目	数学	理科	数学	美術	数学
11.00	三時間目	社会	音楽	英語	国語	理科
12.00	四時間目	理科	国語	理科	英語	社会
1.00	ひるごはん					
1.40	五時間目	英語	数学	美術	数学	美術
2.40	六時間目	美術	社会	特別活動	体育	道徳
3.30	そうじ			ホームルーム		

There is a short break between lessons to allow for movement to the next lesson.

1	時間わり	timetable	3	一時間目　lesson 1 (period 1)
2	組	group, homeroom class	4	とくべつかつどう　special activities

1 マリアナさんの一日のスケジュール
(Mariana's daily schedule)

While Mariana has been living with the Ikeda family, her daily life has been very busy. How does her schedule compare with yours? Note the kanji for o'clock 時 and the kanji for minutes 分.

6時に	おきます。
6時30分に	あさごはんを たべます。
7時から7時30分まで	ピアノを ひきます。
8時に	がっこうに いきます。
8時30分に	ホームルームに いきます。
8時45分に	1時間目のきょうしつに いきます。
9時45分に	2時間目のきょうしつに いきます。（おんがくです。）
10時45分に	3時間目のきょうしつに いきます。（りかです。）
11時45分に	4時間目のきょうしつに いきます。（かていかです。）
12時45分から 1時40分까지では	ひるやすみです。 おべんとうを たべます。
1時40分から 2時40分までは	5時間目のじゅぎょうです。 えいごを べんきょうします。
2時40分から 3時35分までは	6時間目のじゅぎょうです。 （びじゅつです。）
4時に	コンピュータ クラブに いきます。
6時に	うちに かえります。
6時から8時まで	しゅくだいを します。
8時に	ばんごはんを たべます。
9時に	ねます。

1	きょうしつ	classroom	3	ひるやすみ	lunch break, lunchtime
2	じゅぎょう	lesson, class			

アンドルーさんのスケジュール (Andrew's schedule)

Andrew's week, too, is very busy. Fortunately, weekends are a little more relaxed. Remember that, as shown in sentence pattern 32, no marker is needed after general words of time. Which general words could Andrew add to the activities listed? Rewrite each of the new sentences.

General time words

1	よく	often
2	ときどき	sometimes
3	たいてい	usually
4	まいにち	every day
5	いつも	always
6	あさ	in the morning
7	ごご	in the afternoon
8	よる	in the evening
9	ぜんぜん	never (+ negative verb ending)
10	あまり	not very often, not much (+ negative verb ending)

a しんしつを そうじします。

b ともだちの うちに いきます。

c みせに いきます。

d さしみを たべません。

e スナックを たべます。

f サッカーを します。

g べんきょうします。

h にほんごを れんしゅうします。

i ぎんこうへ いきません。

j オーボエを ふきます。

セルフ テスト

1 なんじに おきますか。

2 なんじに ひるごはんを たべますか。

3 たいてい なんじに うちに かえりますか。

4 2じかんめは なんじから なんじまでですか。

5 いつ スポーツを しますか。

6 あさ なんじに がっこうに いきますか。

7 にほんごは どうですか。

8 すしは どうですか。

9 じゅぎょうは なんじに はじまりますか。

10 いま なんじですか。

11 日本語の じゅぎょうは どうですか。

 1 そうじします I/You (will) clean

Outcomes

By the end of this unit, you should be able to:
- describe your leisure activities
- respond to invitations and suggestions
- express specific plans for your leisure time
- describe means of transport and how you get from place to place.

A1

In this unit we see how Andrew, in Osaka, and Mariana, in Tokyo, spend their weekends.

アンドルーさんの会話

1	きんようびのよる	Friday evening	7	おおさかかいゆうかん	Osaka Aquarium
2	いきましょうか	Shall we go?	8	いいアイデア	Good idea
3	どこでも	anywhere	9	どうやって	How?/By what means?
4	どこでもいいです	anywhere would be good	10	えき	(railway) station
5	おおさかじょう	Osaka Castle	11	ちかてつ	the underground
6	ああ、いいですね。	Ooh, that'll be great, won't it?	12	… で	by means of …
			13	あるいて	walking/on foot

1	たこ	kite	6	ピクニック	picnic
2	たこやき	squid dumpling	7	あしたを たのしみにしています	I'm looking forward to tomorrow
3	もっていきましょうか	Shall we take?	8	おやすみなさい	Goodnight (said before going to bed)
4	そうしましょう	Let's do just that			
5	…で	at (following a place where an action occurs)			

A₂ マリアナさんの会話

Mariana's weekends were spent seeing the sights of Tokyo. There was so much to see and do before the end of her stay in Japan.

1	もしもし	Hello (on the telephone)	
2	ビデオ	video	
3	みましょう	Let's watch	
4	いまから	from now	
5	… と	with … (someone)	
6	はらじゅくとぎんざとあきはばら	Harajuku and Ginza and Akihabara (suburbs of Tokyo)	

7	ウィンドウショッピング	window shopping
8	エレクトリックシティ	Electric City
9	かいます	I/You (will) buy
10	わかりません	I'm not sure
11	ねだん	price
12	チェックします	I/You (will) check

覚えましょう
Things teenagers do

There are many things that young people in Japan can do to amuse themselves. There are places to go, things to see, all types of music to listen to. There are also numerous ways of expressing what you will do, and what you want to do. In the following sentence patterns, you will use the ～ましょう ending instead of ～ます.

～ましょう is a polite way of suggesting that someone does something. A polite response is also made using ～ましょう. Use the vocabulary provided to practise the patterns.

Sentence pattern

41

Q (Person 1)

土よう日に　なにを　しましょうか。　What shall we do on Saturday?

A (Person 2)

えいがに　いきましょう。　Let's go to the movies.

コンサート
とうきょうタワー
めいじじんぐう

(Person 1)

ええ、　そうしましょう。　Yes, let's do that.

覚えましょう
Watching . . .

Sentence pattern

42

Q よる　なにを　しましょうか。　What shall we do in the evening?

あさ
ごご

A ビデオを　みましょう。　Let's watch a video.
Q なにを　みましょうか。　What shall we watch?
A 「ものの毛姫」は　どうですか。　What about *Mononokehime*?

1	えいが	movie	4 めいじじんぐう	Meiji Shrine
2	コンサート	concert	5 もののけ毛姫	*Mononokehime* — a popular
3	とうきょうタワー	Tokyo Tower		Japanese animated movie

B 3 覚えましょう
Listening …

Sentence pattern

43

Q よる なにを しましょうか。 　What shall we do in the evening?

A CDを ききましょう。 　Let's listen to a CD.

B 4 覚えましょう
Other recreational activities

Sentence pattern

44

Q あさ 何を しましょうか。 　What shall we do in the morning?

A かいものに いきましょう。 　Let's go shopping.

えんそく
ピクニック
つり
さんぽ
ジョギング
はなみ
スキー

C 1 During Mariana and Andrew's stay in Tokyo and Osaka respectively, they were able to go to many fascinating places—some very old and culturally significant, some new and very 'high-tech', and some that blend the old and the new.

You can surf the Web and read travel books and brochures for details about popular haunts of the young (and not so young) in Japan. Andrew and Mariana's photos taken during their time there will help you get some ideas about where you might want to go.

マリアナさんのしゃしん

日本について Harajuku is one of Tokyo's most fashionable areas, with several of Japan's top clothing designers having their headquarters and boutiques in the area. The streets are lined with countless clothing shops. The flea market near Harajuku Station is popular with the young, particularly girls looking for bargains in ornaments and accessories. Open-air discos are held on Sundays. These provide an opportunity for young Japanese to let their hair down, express their individuality and share their talents.

1	ききましょう	let's listen (to)	5 つり	fishing
2	かいものに いきましょう	let's go shopping	6 さんぽ	walk, stroll
3	…に	for the purpose of/for/on	7 ジョギング	jogging
			8 はなみ	flower viewing
4	えんそく	day excursion	9 スキー	skiing

日本について

ぎんざ

Ginza means 'Silver Mint' and is so named because it was the site of a silver mint in 1612. It became the first place in Japan to be modernised and to display goods from outside Japan.

The Ginza is reputed to be one of the most expensive shopping locations in the world. It is an area of some six hectares of shops, expensive boutiques, galleries and restaurants. While its prices make most items unaffordable for the average tourist, it is certainly worth a visit. Its trademark street lamps, shady trees, exquisite store windows and its 'no-car' day on Sunday make a visit a memorable experience.

ぎんざの　デパート

とうきょうの　エレクトリックシティー　あきはばら

日本について

あきはばら

Akihabara is best known for its street upon street of shops—all selling electrical and electronic goods. Hours can be spent browsing over the latest technological gimmicks and gadgetry, and the newest in computers and computer software. Whitegoods (washing machines, fridges and so on) can be found in a host of matching colours—blues, purples, pinks, yellows. What adds to the excitement of shopping here is the opportunity to bargain. The vendors on footpaths inviting bargain hunters, and the bright and colourful signs, all add to the festive feel of this suburb.

日本について

めいじじんぐう

The Meiji Shrine is dedicated to the Emperor and Empress Meiji, who were responsible for the modernisation of Japan by opening it to the outside world 150 years ago. Meiji Jingu (Shrine) was opened in 1920, with its current buildings constructed in the Shinto architectural style in 1958. Meiji Jingu is within a short walking distance of the main Harajuku thoroughfare.

めいじじんぐう

アンドルーさんのしゃしん

日本について

おおさかかいゆうかん

The Osaka 'Ring of Fire' Aquarium recreates the diverse environments found along the continuous zone of seismic and volcanic activity around the Pacific Ocean. The myriad creatures found at each site—including the Japan Forest, the Gulf of Panama, the coast of Chile, Antarctica, the Tasman Sea and the Great Barrier Reef—can be viewed from amazing proximity.

おおさかかいゆうかん

日本について

おおさかじょう

Osaka Castle is a modern reconstruction, on a much smaller scale, of the original castle built in 1585. It commands an extensive view of the city and is home to Osaka Castle Museum. The history of this castle is told through 3D stereoscopic and panoramic dioramas and artefacts on each level of the building.

おおさかじょう

日本について

アメリカむら

Osaka has many quite distinct shopping districts. Within the district called Shinsaibashi, there are hundreds of shops and major department stores such as Daimaru, Sogo and Takashimaya. On the east side of this shopping arcade is another shopping centre called ヨーロッパむら (European Village). On the west side is another arcade called アメリカむら (American Village). Amerika Mura is particularly popular with young people who want to get a taste of America and look 'trendy' in American clothes.

アメリカむら

Leisure pursuits

There are plenty of activities to engage in and places to see in Japan. How would you answer the questions about the places shown?

1 あした　はなみに　いきましょうか。

2 あした　がっこうに　いきましょうか。

3 ディズニーランドに　いきましょうか。

4 ライオンキングを　みましょうか。

5 かいものに　いきましょうか。

6 CDを　ききましょうか。

7 えきへ　いきましょうか。

8 きょうとタワーに　いきましょうか。

9 すしを　たべましょうか。

10 ファーストキッチンへ　いきましょうか。
（ファーストキッチンで　たべましょうか。）

What's the difference between these two questions? Which one would you be more likely to use?

覚えましょう
With whom?

On your first trip to Japan, you might be a little hesitant about venturing out alone. The next sentence pattern will be useful in clarifying with whom you will be going out.

Sentence pattern

45

Q だれと こうえんに いきますか。	With whom are we going to the park?
A おかあさんと いきます。	We will go with Mum.
A ひとりで いきます。	I'm going by myself.

Explanation

In this pattern, と means 'with' and it goes after the name of the person with whom you do something. Look at these examples:

例 おかあさんと   with Mum
ゆうこさんと   with Yuko

When asking someone with whom they do something, use the phrase だれと meaning 'with whom?':

だれ ＋ と   with whom?
(who) (with)

Who, and/or how many people are taking part in these activities?

ひとりで ジョギングに いきます。

おかあさんと おとうさんと テレビを みます。

たろうくんは 一ねんせいと しゅうがく りょこうに いきます。

ともだちと ビデオを みます。

I	だれと	With whom?	3	しゅうがくりょこう	school excursion (see page 74)
2	こうえん	park	4	みます	I/You (will) see, watch

F 覚えましょう
Transport

Japan has an amazing network of public transport. (You can access a wealth of information about the types of transport on the Internet.) Using buses, trains, the underground, the 'bullet train', taxis and bikes is a regular occurrence for most Japanese commuting to work or to school and home again. The next sentence pattern shows how you can explain what means of transport you use to get somewhere.

Sentence pattern

46

Q	どうやって　いきますか。		How will we go? (How will we get there?)
A	ちかてつで　いきます。		We'll go by the subway.

means of transport + で	+	verb いきます。	(I'll) go by (means of transport).

Explanation

で has several uses and meanings . You have previously used it as a meaning marker denoting the place of action. In this context, when it follows a means of transport, it means 'by means of'.

G ## のりもの (Means of transport)

どうやって　いきますか。

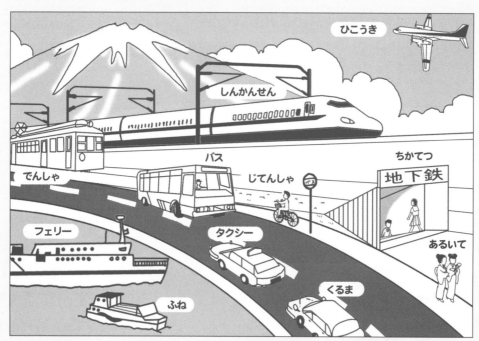

1	のりもの	(means of) transport, vehicles	4	でんしゃ	train/tram	8	ひこうき	plane
			5	しんかんせん	'bullet' train	9	あるいて	on foot
2	くるま	car	6	ちかてつ	underground, subway	10	じてんしゃ	bicycle
3	バス	bus	7	タクシー	taxi	11	ふね	boat, ship
						12	フェリー	ferry

H Andrew's and Mariana's photos give some idea of the many ways in which people get around. List the means of transport shown in the photographs.

覚えましょう
From where to where?

Sentence pattern

47

Q しんじゅくから　ぎんざまで
どうやって　いきますか。

How do you go from Shinjuku
to the Ginza?

A ちかてつで　いきます。

I go by (means of) the underground.

Explanation

In sentence pattern 38 on page 139, you learned how you can use the meaning markers
… から (from) and … まで (until/as far as/to). Now you can combine から, まで and
どうやって to ask how to get from one place to another.

J

In just one day in Tokyo, you could use at least five modes of transport. Follow Mariana's route
from the Ikeda home to the various places she visits with Yoko. Explain how she will go **from** he
home **to** each place and back home again, using the various means of transport shown.

例　うちから　えきまで　じてんしゃで　いきます。

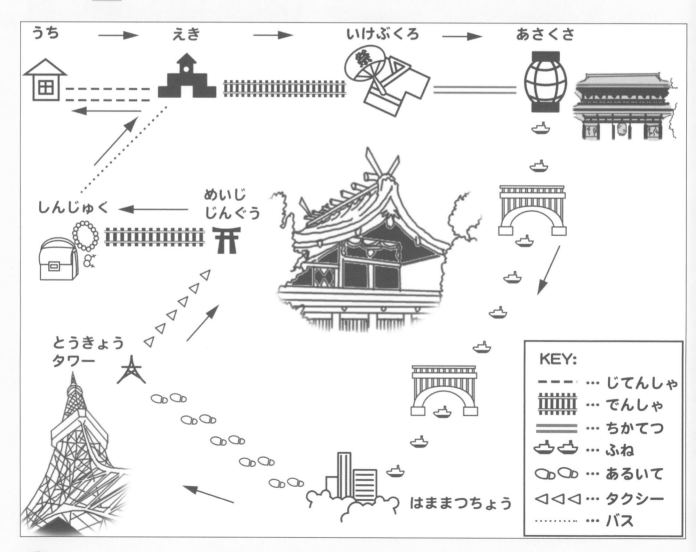

K

Imagine that you are going to Japan. You will travel in stages as shown below.

You leave a note with your Japanese teacher detailing all your movements on Day 1. What do you write for the following stages?

1 From your home city to Narita by plane by yourself

2 From Narita Airport by NEX (Narita Express train) to Ueno with your host family

3 From Ueno to Shibuya by train with your host family

4 From Shibuya to a restaurant with your host family by taxi

5 From the restaurant to home with your host family on foot

L

10

11

12

セルフ テスト

1 だれと がっこうに いきますか。

2 キックボードを しますか。

3 うちから がっこうまで どうやって いきますか。

4 ときどき ピクニックに いきますか。

5 ともだちと つりに いきますか。

6 なんよう日に えいがを みましょうか。

7 よる たいてい なにを しますか。

9 おたんじょう日に たいてい レストランで たべますか。
うちで たべますか。

10 らいねん おおさかかいゆうかんに いきますか。

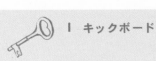

Grammar guide

A Japanese sentence follows a set pattern and conforms to set rules. This makes Japanese grammar quite easy compared with other languages. You just keep adding to a basic structure to make the sentence more complex. The following grammar guide shows how each sentence pattern introduced in *Tsumiki 1* is based on an easy-to-learn system of language items added together with a verb at the end.

Before you put any language item before the verb, take care to ensure that the correct 'meaning marker' is attached to the language item (if one is necessary). In summary, a Japanese sentence looks like this, with a main verb or verb-type ending at the end:

| language item A
? + MM | + | language item B
? + MM | + | language item C
? + MM | + | main verb or verb-type ending
?。 |

MM represents a meaning marker (such as は、が、で、に、の、へ、と、まで、から).

Part A: Statements

Model 1　　It is A; I am A; You are A

| language item A
? | + | verb-type ending
です。 |

Examples　　*Pages*

a	しちがつ 七月です。	It is (in) July.	*121*
b	いちじです。	It is one o'clock.	*136*
c	にじはんです。	It is half past two.	*137*
d	しちじごふんです。	It is five past seven.	*137*
e	くじじゅっぷんまえです。	It is ten to nine.	*137*
f	おいしいです。	It's delicious.	*113*
g	すずき　みえこさんです。	She is Mieko Suzuki.	*32*
h	ハンサムです。	He is handsome.	*134*
i	ちゅうごくじんです。	I am Chinese.	*35*

Model 2　　A is B

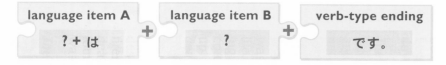

| language item A
? + は | + | language item B
? | + | verb-type ending
です。 |

は means 'as for', 'as far as such-and-such or so-and-so is concerned'.
は marks the language item that is the topic of the sentence.
Because です means 'is', 'am' or 'are', it links one thing with another. It is used to say that one thing is another.

Examples

| a | わたしは　アンドルーです。 | I am Andrew. | 32 |
| b | アンドルーくんは　オーストラリアじんです。 | Andrew is Australian. | 38 |

c おかあさんは 四十五さいです。 Mum is 45 years of age. 46

d ジョンくんは 八ねんせいです。 John is in Year 8. 51

e いちばんすきなかもくは すうがくです。 My favourite subject is Maths. 75

f かぞくは 五人です。 There are five people in my family. (My family is a 5-person family.) 81

g おとうさんは けんちくかです。 My father is an architect. 82

h これは すしです。 This is sushi. 104

i これは すしじゃないです。 This is not sushi. 112

This example uses the negative form of です（じゃないです）。

j ようかんは あまいです。 Yokan is sweet. 113

k マリアナさんは たつどしです。 Mariana was born in the Year of the Dragon. 125

Model 3   A lives in/at B

language item A		language item B		verb
? + は	+	**? + に**	+	**すんでいます。**

Example

マリアナさんは オークランドに すんでいます。 Mariana lives in Auckland. 38

Model 4   Ownership: A's B; the B of A

language item A		language item B		other language items and a verb
? + の	+	**?**	+	

Examples

a こうべの すみよしに すんでいます。 I/You live in Sumiyoshi in Kobe. 38

b えみさんは ちゅうがっこうの いちねんせいです。 Emi is a first year student of/in a junior high school. (Emi is a junior high school's first year student.) 52

c わたしの でんわばんごうは 02 5964 2238です。 My telephone number is 02 5964 2238. 52

d ねこの なまえは「くろ」です。 The cat's name is 'Blacky'. 87

e わたしの ほんです。 It is my book. 108

f わたしの ほんじゃないです。 It is not my book. 108

Model 5   (Person) lives in A in B; (Person) lives in the suburb of A in the city of B

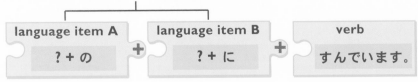

double language item

language item A		language item B		verb
? + の	+	**? + に**	+	**すんでいます。**

Example

こうべの すみよしに すんでいます。 I/You live in Sumiyoshi in Kobe. 38

Model 6　　(Person) does/is doing/does not/is not doing B

Examples　　　　　　　　　　　　　　　　　　　　　　　　　　　　　　*Pages*

a	ようこさんは　たっきゅうを　します。	Yoko plays table tennis.	57, 60
b	フルートを　ふきます。	I/You play the flute.	62
c	にほんごを　ならっています。	I/You am learning Japanese.	63
d	チェスを　しません。	I/You don't play chess.	63
e	しゃかいを　べんきょうしていません。	I/You don't study/I am/You are not studying Social Studies.	72
f	すしを　たべます。	I/You eat/will eat sushi.	94

Model 7　　Let's do ...

The activity being proposed could be presented as an object plus verb, as in examples **a** and **b**, or as a single verb, as in examples **c** and **d**.

Examples

a	ビデオを　みましょう。	Let's watch a video.	146
b	CDを　ききましょう。	Let's listen to a CD.	146
c	そうしましょう。	Let's do that.	146
d	いきましょう。	Let's go.	146

Model 8　　(Person) doesn't like A

Examples

りかは　すきじゃないです。	I/You don't like Science.	75

Model 9　　(Person) likes A

language item A　　?＋が　＋　verb-type ending　すきです。

Examples

りかが　すきです。	I/You like Science.	75

Model 10   A works/is working in/at place B

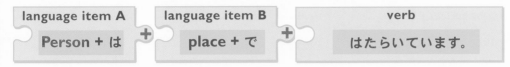

で in this pattern indicates a place where an action occurs.

Examples   *Pages*

おとうさんは　かいしゃで　はたらいています。   My father works/is working in
                                                      a company.   84

Model 11   A has/keeps C (a number and animal counter) of animal B

Examples

a　けんすけくんは　ねこを　一匹_{いっぴき}　かっています。   Kensuke has one cat.   85
b　ペットを　かっていません。   I/You don't have a pet.   85

Model 12   Could I please have A

Examples

すしを　ください。   Could I please have some sushi.   94

Model 13   (Person) eats/I eat B for meal A

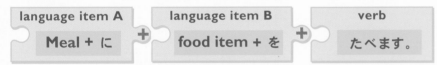

In this pattern, に means 'for'. The emphasis is on the food you eat, not on the meal time. If you want to emphasise the meal time (for example, 'For lunch, I don't eat cereal'), use は instead of に.

Example

あさごはんに　トーストを　たべます。   I eat toast for breakfast.   97

Model 14   A goes/is going/will go to place B

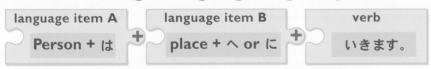

へ always means 'to'. に also means 'to' but on some occasions it has other meanings, as in model 13 above, where it means 'for'. It can also be used to mean 'for the purpose of'. If you wish to indicate who is going somewhere, add language item A.

Example

えみさんは　にほんへ　いきます。   Emi is going to Japan.   100

Model 15   A too is going/will go to place B

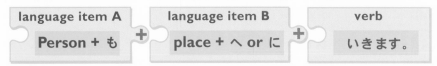

language item A	language item B	verb
Person + も	place + へ or に	いきます。

Example   *Pages*

わたしも　にほんへ　いきます。   I am going to Japan too.   *100*

Model 16   A is/means 'C' in language B

language item A	language item B	language item C	verb-type ending
? + は	language + で	'?'	です。

In this pattern, で is used to indicate 'in'.

Example

さしみは　えいごで「ローフィッシュ」です。   Sashimi is 'raw fish' in English.   *110*

Model 17   The action in (B+) C occurs with the frequency in A

language item A	language item B	verb C
General time	? + を or ? + へ/に	?。

When giving the general time at which a specific action will occur, no extra meaning marker is necessary unless you are being quite emphatic about the time. This is easy to remember when we think that in English we don't say 'on tomorrow' or 'at sometimes'. Nor do the Japanese.

Examples

a   あした　パーティーを　しません。   I am not having a party tomorrow.   *127*

b   いつも　スナックを　たべます。   I always eat snacks.   *142*

c   よる　にほんごを　れんしゅうします。   I practise Japanese at night.   *142*

d   ぜんぜん　ぎんこうへ　いきません。   I never go to the bank.   *142*

e   あまり　さしみを　たべません。   I don't eat sashimi very often.   *142*

Model 18   The action in (B+) C occurs with the frequency in A

language item A	language item B	verb C
Specific time + に	? + を	?。

When you are being specific about when an activity will occur, use meaning marker に meaning 'at' or 'on'. As shown in examples **b** and **c**, the action may be expressed as one verb.

Examples

a   土よう日に　パーティーを　します。   I am/You are having a party
                                            on Saturday.   *128*

b   6じはんに　おきます。   (I) get up at 6.30.   *138*

c   9じに　はじまります。   It starts at 9.00.   *138*

Model 19   (Person)/I will become age B in time A

language item A		language item B		verb
Specific time + に	**+**	**age + に**	**+**	**なります。**

Examples   *Pages*

じゅういちがつ　　さい
十一月に　十四才に　なります。   I will become (turn) 14 years of age
　　　　　　　　　　　　　　　　　　　　　　　　　in November.   *129*

Model 20   (To do C) from A to B; from time A to time B; from place A to place B

language item A		language item B		verb C
? + から	**+**	**? + まで**	**+**	**?。**

The action may be expressed as an object plus verb as shown in **a**, or as one verb as shown in **b**.

Examples

しち　　　く
a　7じから　9じはんまで　しゅくだいを　します。   I/You do homework from 7.00
　　　　　　　　　　　　　　　　　　　　　　　　　until 9.30.   *139*

b　とうきょうから　おおさかまで　いきます。   I/You will go from Tokyo to Osaka.   *139*

Model 21   Let's go (to do) activity A

language item A		verb
Activity + に	**+**	**いきましょう。**

Examples

a　えいがに　いきましょう。   Let's go to a movie.   *146*
b　めいじじんぐうに　いきましょう。   Let's go to Meiji Shrine.   *146*
c　かいものに　いきましょう。   Let's go shopping.   *147*
d　つりに　いきましょう。   Let's go fishing.   *147*
e　さんぽに　いきましょう。   Let's go for a walk.   *147*

Model 22   (Person) does B with person A

language item A		verb B
Person + と	**+**	**?。**

Examples

おかあさんと　いきます。   I'll go with Mum.   *151*
Note: ひとりで　いきます。   I'll go by myself.   *151*

Model 23　　To go by means of A (transport)

language item A		verb
Transport + で	**+**	**いきます。**

Examples   *Pages*

ちかてつで　いきます。   We'll go by subway.   *152*

Note: to say that you go 'by foot', 'on foot' or 'walk', Japanese use the compound verb あるいていきます which literally means 'I go walking'.

Part B: Questions

A question can be constructed by adding か to a sentence. For example:

やきゅうを　します。   I play baseball.

やきゅうを　しますか。   Do you play baseball?   *57*

Many other questions are formed using 'question words' such as 'what' (なに or なん), 'where' (どこ), 'when' (いつ), 'who' (だれ), 'how' (どうやって or どう) and 'what kind of' (どんな). The following examples provide a summary of how these question words can be used.

I　　What?　　なに or なん

(Note that 'what' is sometimes pronounced なに and sometimes なん as shown in examples below. If it is written in kanji, it is always 何.

a	（お）なまえは　なんですか？	What is your/his/her name?	*32*
b	（あなたは）なんさいですか。	How old are you?	*46*
c	（あなたは）なんねんせいですか。	What year/grade are you in at school?	*51*
d	でんわばんごうは　なんばんですか。	What is your telephone number?	*52*
e	なにを　べんきょうしていますか。	What are you studying?	*72*
f	いちばんすきな　かもくは　なんですか。	What is your favourite subject?	*75*
g	ごかぞくは　なん人ですか。	How many people are there in your family?	*81*
h	なん人　かぞくですか。	How many people are there in your family?	*81*
i	おとうさんの　ごしょくぎょうは　なんですか。	What is your father's occupation?	*82*
j	なにを　たべますか。	What will/do you eat?	*94*
k	あさごはんに　なにを　たべますか。	What do/will you eat for breakfast?	*97*
l	それは　なんですか。	What is that?	*104*
m	「さしみ」は　えいごで　なんですか。	What is sashimi in English?	*110*
n	おたんじょう日は　なん月ですか。	What month is your birthday?	*121*
o	なん日ですか。	What day of the month is it?	*122*
p	なんよう日ですか。	What day of the week is it?	*123*
q	なにどしですか。	What is your Chinese zodiac sign?	*125*
r	なんですか。	What is it?	*126*
s	なんよう日に　パーティーを　しますか。	On what day are you having a party?	*128*
t	いま　なんじですか。	What time is it now?	*136, 137 & 139*
u	なんじに　うちに　かえりますか。	At what time will you return home?	*138*
v	土よう日に　なにを　しましょうか。	What shall we do on Saturday?	*146*

Glossary Japanese–English

あ

ああ、いいですね	Ooh, that'll be great, won't it?	143
あいきどう	aikido (a martial art)	59
あいます	(I/You) (will) meet (verb)	76
あきはばら	Akihabara (suburb of Tokyo)	145
あけて	Open it up! (informal) (verb)	116
あけてください	Please open it (verb)	118
あさ	(in the) morning	132, 142
あさごはん	breakfast	97
あした	tomorrow	117, 128
あしたをたのしみに しています	I'm looking forward to tomorrow	144
あとで	after, later	92
アデレード	Adelaide	39
あなたは?	(What about) you?	30
あひる	duck	86
アフリカ	Africa	37
あまい	sweet (adj.)	113
あまり … ません	not often, not much	142
あまり じょうずじゃ ないです	I'm not very good at it	76
アメリカ	America	37
アメリカじん	American (person)	37
ありがとうございました	Thank you very much (for what you have done)	31
ありがとうございます	Thanks (very much)	31
あるいて	walking, on foot	143, 152
あれ	that over there	103
アンケート	survey (noun)	WB38
アンドルーさんの かいわ	Andrew's conversation	30
アンドルー マクドナルド	Andrew McDonald	30

い

いい	good	134
いいアイデア	good idea	143
いいえ	no	35
いいえ、そんなことは ないです	No, that is not so/Not at all (A polite way of saying 'I'm not very good')	56
いいえ、よろこんで	No, not at all. We are delighted (to be able to host you)	102
いかがですか	How is it?	113
いきましょうか	Shall we go? (verb)	143
いきます	(I/You) go (verb)	92
イギリス	England	37
イギリスじん	English (person)	37
いけばな	flower arrangement	105
いしゃ	doctor	78
いす	chair	109
いただきます	I humbly receive (said before meals)	WB 18
イタリア	Italy	37
イタリアご	Italian (language)	63

イタリアじん	Italian (person)	37
いち (一)	one	44
いちがつ	January	121
いちじかんめ	Lesson 1 (Period 1)	140
いちねんせい	first-year student	42
いちばんすきなかもく	favourite subject	68
いつ	when	117
いつか	fifth (day of the month)	122
いっさい	one year old	44
いってきます	See you again (I'm going and I shall come back)	40
いってらっしゃい	Goodbye (Go and please come back)	40
いっぴき	one small animal	85
いつも	always	142
いぬ	dog	78
いぬどし	Year of the Dog	125
いのしし	wild boar, pig	125
いのししどし	Year of the Pig	125
いま	now	128
いまから	from now	145
いもうと	younger sister	78
いもうと (さん)	(your) younger sister	80
イラン	Iran	37
イランじん	Iranian (person)	37
いろいろ	various	97
インドネシア	Indonesia	36
インドネシアご	Indonesian (language)	63
インドネシアじん	Indonesian (person)	36

う

ウアー！	scream of person falling from a great height	WB15
ウィンドウショッピング	window shopping	145
ウエイトレス	waitress	82
ウェリントン	Wellington	39
ウォークマン	Walkman	119
うさぎ	rabbit	125
うさぎどし	Year of the Rabbit	116, 125
うし	cow, ox	125
うしどし	Year of the Ox	125
うち	home, house	84
うちの いぬ	family dog	107
うちの かぞくです	this is our family	102
うちの ねこ	family cat	115
うちます	(I/You) play (a musical instrument: percussion (lit. beat)) (verb)	62
うに	sea urchin	97
うま	horse	86
うまどし	Year of the Horse	125
うめだ スカイビル	Umeda Sky Building	129
うれしい	(I'm so) happy/(I'm so) glad (adj.)	116
うん	yes (informal)	131

え

え？	What?	42
エアコンのリモコン	air conditioner remote control	106
えいが	movie	146
えいご	English (language)	56
えいごで	in/by means of English	103
ええ	yeah	55
えき	(railway) station	143
エジプト	Egypt	37
エジプトじん	Egyptian (person)	37
エレクトリックシティ	Electric City	145
えんげき	Speech and Drama (school subject)	71
えんそく	excursion	147
えんぴつ	pencil	108

お

(お) たんじょうび	(your/someone's) birthday	116
おいしい	delicious (adj.)	113
おいしそう	looks delicious	134
おいしそうですね	It looks delicious	126
オークランド	Auckland	31
おおさかかいゆうかん	Osaka Aquarium	143
おおさかじょう	Osaka Castle	143
オーストラリア	Australia	36
オーストラリアじん	Australian (person)	36
オーボエ	oboe	62
おかあさん	mother	43
おかえりなさい	(Ah!) You've returned	78
おかし	sweets, confectionery	112
おきます	(I/You) get up (out of bed) (verb)	137
おげんきですか	How are you?	64
おしい	You're close!/You just missed!	126
おじいさん	grandfather	80
おじさん	uncle	80
おたんじょう日、おめでとうございます	Happy birthday	116
おちゃ	tea	94
おとうさん	father	43
おとうと	younger brother	47
おとうと (さん)	(your) younger brother	80
おなじ	same	132
おなじくらい	about the same	132
おなじですね	It's the same (for both of us), isn't it?	68
おなまえは？	What is your name?	31
おに	devil	87
おにいさん	older brother	79
おねえさん	older sister	76
おのみものは？	Would you like a drink?	93
おばあさん	grandmother	78
おばさん	aunty	80
おはつ てんじん	Ohatsu Tenjin Shrine	129
おはようございます	Good morning	30
オフィス	office	84
おべんとう	Boxed lunch	97
おぼえかた	how to remember	41
おめでとうございます	congratulations	118
おもしろい	interesting (adj.)	134
おもしろそう	looks interesting	126
おやすみなさい	goodnight	144
おりがみ	origami (paper folding)	61

オレンジジュース	orange juice	94
おわります	(something) ends (verb)	132, 137
おん	(Chinese reading or pronunciation of kanji)	35
おんがく	Music (school subject)	68

か

… か	(used at the end of a statement to turn a statement into a question)	35
… が	but, however	64
カード	card	WB42
がいこくご	foreign language	71
かいしゃ	company	84
かいしゃいん	company employee	79
かいて ください	Please write (verb)	40
かいます	(I/You)(will) buy (verb)	145
かいもの	shopping (verb)	147
かいものに いきましょう	Let's go shopping	147
かえります	(I/You)(will) return (home) (verb)	131, 137
かがく	Chemistry (school subject)	71
かきかた	how to write	35
がくせい	student	82
かけいず	family tree	19
かけじく	scroll hanging in a tokonoma	105
かぞく	family	78
ガタガタ	rattle, clatter	WB15
カチカチ	(sound of) clock ticking	WB15
かっこいい	cool, attractive, trendy (adj.)	134
がっこう	school	68, 79
かっています	keep, care for (pet) (verb)	78
かていか	Home Economics (school subject)	71
カナダ	Canada	37
カナダじん	Canadian (person)	37
カナリア	canary	87
かまぼこ	steamed fish-paste cake	110
かみだな	household Shinto altar	105
かようび	Tuesday	123
… から …まで	from … to …	132
からて	karate (a martial art)	55
カルタ	traditional Japanese playing-cards	61
カルピスソーダ	Calpis soda	93
かわいい	cute (adj.)	88, 134
かんこく	Korea	36
かんこくご	Korean (language)	63
かんこくじん	Korean (person)	36
かんごふ	nurse	79
がんばって!	Stick at it!/Persist!	93
かんぶん	Chinese Literature (school subject)	71

き

ききましょう	let's listen (verb)	147
ぎじゅつ	Manual Arts (school subject)	71
ぎじゅつ - かてい	Industrial Arts and Homemaking	71
ギター	guitar	62
きちょう	captain, pilot	82
キックボード	scooter	155
キックボードをします	(I/You) ride a scooter (verb)	155
きっさてん	coffee shop	84
きます	(I/You) (will) come (verb)	137
きみ	you (used by males)	35
キャア	shout, scream	WB15

し

す

せ

そ

みます | (I/You) (will) see, watch | 151
みんな | everyone | 69

む

むいか | sixth (day of the month) | 122
むしゃむしゃ | (sound of) munching, devouring | WB28
むしょく | unemployed | 82
むずかしい | difficult (adj.) | 131

め

めいじじんぐう | Meiji Shrine | 146
メルボルン | Melbourne | 39

も

… も | … also | 91
もういちど いって ください | Please say it once more | 40
もくようび | Thursday | 123
もしもし | Hello (on the telephone) | 145
もちろん | of course | 69
… もっていきましょうか | Shall we take …? | 144
ものほしざお | clothes line (Japanese-style) | 106
モルモット | guinea pig | 86

や

… や … | and … (so on) | 68
やきそば | fried noodles (like 'chow mein') | 110
やきゅう | baseball | 57, 58
ヤクルト | Yakult (a drink) | WB83
やすみ | holiday | 93

よ

… よ | (placed at the end of a sentence to add emphasis) | 117
ようか | eighth (day of the month) | 122
ようかん | sweet bean jelly | 113
ようこさんの でんわばんごう | Yoko's telephone number | 42
ようこそ | Welcome | 102
ようしょく | western-style food | 94
よく | often | 142
よっか | fourth (day of the month) | 122
よにん | four people | 81
… より | from … (at the end of a letter) | 64
よる | (in the) evening, (at) night | 131
よろしく | (I'm) glad to meet you | 51
よん、し（四） | four | 44
よんさい | four years of age | 44
よんじゅう | forty | 44
よんじゅっさい | forty years of age | 44
よんひき | four small animals | 85

ら

ラーメン | Chinese noodles | 110
らいしゅう | next week | 117
らいねん | next year | 128
らくに してください | Please relax | 91

り

りか | Science (school subject) | 68, 71
りか だいいちぶんや | Integrated Science (school subject) | 71
りくじょう | track and field | 59
りょくちゃ | green tea | 94

れ

れい | example | 35
れきし | History (school subject) | 71
レスリング | wrestling | 59
レモネード | lemonade | 94
れんしゅう | practice (noun) | 76
れんしゅうしてください | Please practise | 127
れんしゅうします | (I/You) (will) practise (verb) | 69

ろ

ロースト | roast | 110
ろく（六） | six | 44
ろくがつ | June | 121
ろくさい | six years of age | 44
ろくじゅう | sixty | 44
ろくじゅっさい | sixty years of age | 44
ろくにん | six people | 81
ロシア | Russia | 36
ロシアじん | Russian (person) | 36

わ

わあ！すごい！ | Wow, this is fantastic! | 119
わあー、びっくりした！ | Wow, what a surprise! | 118
わかりません | I don't understand, I'm not sure | 91, 145
わしょく | Japanese-style food | 91
わたし | I/me | 30
わたしたちの マンション | our unit, apartment | 103
わたしの でんわばんごう | my telephone number | 52
わたし (は) | I | 30
わたしも | I too, me too | 92

Glossary English–Japanese

A

Adelaide	アデレード	39
Africa	アフリカ	36
after, later	あとで	91
after lessons (after school)	じゅぎょうの あとで	69
after that	そのあと	129
afternoon (in the)	ごご	142
aikido	あいきどう	59
air conditioner remote control	エアコンのリモコン	106
... also, too	... も	91
always	いつも	142
America	アメリカ	37
American (person)	アメリカじん	37
and	そして	102
and (in a list)	... と ...	55
and ... (so on)	... や ...	68
animal	どうぶつ	86
animal (counter)	... ひき (匹)	85
anything	なんでも	114
anywhere	どこでも	143
apartment, unit	マンション	103
April	しがつ (四月)	121
architect	けんちくか	82
architect's office	けんちくじむしょ	115
Arithmetic (school subject)	さんすう	71
Armed forces, member of	ぐんじん	82
arrive (verb)	つきます	137
Art (school subject)	びじゅつ	71
at ... (following a place where an action occurs)	... で	84, 144
August	はちがつ (八月)	121
aunty	おばさん	80
Australia	オーストラリア	36
Australian (person)	オーストラリアじん	36
awful/poor tasting (adj.)	まずい	113

B

bank	ぎんこう	84
baseball	やきゅう	57
basketball	バスケットボール	55
bathroom	ふろば	106
beautiful	きれい	126
become, will become (verb)	なります	117
bedroom	しんしつ	109
beer	ビール	94
before	まえ	139
before lessons (before school)	じゅぎょうの まえに	69
begins (something begins) (verb)	はじまります	132, 137
bicycle	じてんしゃ	152
Biology (school subject)	せいぶつ	71
bird	とり	86
birthday	たんじょうび	116

birthday, (your/someone's) birthday	（お）たんじょうび	116
bit, a	ちょっと	133
black	くろ	89
blanket	ブランケット	99
blood group	けつえきがた	WB108
blow, play (a musical instrument) (verb)	ふきます	62
boar, wild pig	いのしし	125
book	ほん	108
boxed lunch	おべんとう	97
boxing	ボクシング	59
bread	パン	112
Brazil	ブラジル	37
Brazilian (person)	ブラジルじん	37
breakfast	あさごはん	97
Brisbane	ブリスベン	39
brother		
– older brother	おにいさん	79
– younger brother	おとうと	47, 80
bullet train	しんかんせん	152
bus	バス	152
Business Principles	しょうぎょうぼき	71
but, however	が、けど、でも	55, 64, 134
buy (verb)	かいます	145
by means of (transport)	... で	143
by myself/yourself/ourselves	ひとりで	145

C

cabbage	キャベツ	WB81
Calligraphy (school subject)	しょどう	71
Calpis soda	カルピスソーダ	93
Canada	カナダ	37
Canadian (person)	カナダじん	37
canary	カナリア	87
Canberra	キャンベラ	39
captain, pilot	きちょう	82
car	くるま	152
cards (playing cards)	トランプ	99
carpenter	だいく	82
cat	ねこ	86
cereal	シリアル	100
chair	いす	109
check (verb)	チェックします	145
Chemistry (school subject)	かがく	71
chess	チェス	61
chicken, fowl	にわとり	86
China	ちゅうごく	36
Chinese (language)	ちゅうごくご	63
Chinese (person)	ちゅうごくじん	36
chocolate	チョコレート	118
clarinet	クラリネット	62
classroom	きょうしつ	141
clean (verb)	そうじします	142

cleaning (*noun*)	そうじ	133
clothes line (Japanese-style)	ものほしざお	106
club	クラブ	133
Coca-Cola	コカコーラ	94
coffee	コーヒー	94
coffee shop	きっさてん	84
come (*verb*)	きます	137
Commerce (school subject)	しょうぎょうぼき	71
company	かいしゃ	84
company employee	かいしゃいん	79
compulsory subjects	ひっしゅうかもく (必修科目)	WB63
computer game	コンピュータゲーム	61
computer programmer	コンピュータのプログラマー	78
Computing (school subject)	コンピュータ、じょうほう	71
concert	コンサート	146
congratulations	おめでとうございます	118
cool, attractive, trendy (*adj.*)	かっこいい	134
cool, terrific (*adj.*)	すごい	103
correct (*adj.*)	ただしい	WB96
cow, ox	うし	125
cram school	じゅく	131
cricket	クリケット	55
cushion (for sitting on the floor)	ざぶとん	105
cute (*adj.*)	かわいい	88, 134

D

Darwin	ダーウィン	39
December	じゅうにがつ (十二月)	121
delicious (*adj.*)	おいしい	113
dentist	はいしゃ	82
department store	デパート	84
desk, table	つくえ	105
devil	おに	87
difficult (*adj.*)	むずかしい	131
dinner	ばんごはん	97
Disneyland	ディズニーランド	150
do, play (*verb*)	します	55
doctor	いしゃ	78
dog	いぬ	78
dragon	たつ	125
drink (*noun*)	のみもの	93
drink (*verb*)	のみます	93
drums (Japanese-style)	たいこ	62
duck	あひる	86

E

eat (*verb*)	たべます	91
egg	たまご	112
Egypt	エジプト	37
Egyptian (person)	エジプトじん	37
eight	はち (八)	44
eighty	はちじゅう (八十)	44
electronic dictionary	でんしじしょ	119
elective subjects	せんたくかもく (選択科目)	WB63
elementary school primary school	しょうがっこう	52
eleven	じゅういち (十一)	44
ends (something ends) (*verb*)	おわります	132, 137
England	イギリス	37
English (language)	えいご	56

English (person)	イギリスじん	37
enjoyable, fun (*adj.*)	たのしい	133
entrance, front entry to a home	げんかん	103, 106
evening (in the)	よる	131
every day	まいにち	142
everyone	みなさん、みんな	30, 69
everyone in the class	クラスの みんな	131
example	れい	35
excellent, really good (*adj.*)	すごくいい	126
excursion	えんそく	147
Excuse me, but …	すみませんが …	91

F

factory	こうじょう	84
family	かぞく	78
– your family	ごかぞく	78
family cat	うちの ねこ	115
family dog	うちの いぬ	107
family tree	かけいず	19
Fanta	ファンタ	94
fantastic (*adj.*)	すごい	126
father	おとうさん	43
father's	おとうさんの	78
favourite subject	いちばんすきなかもく	68
February	にがつ (二月)	121
ferry	フェリー	152
fifty	ごじゅう (五十)	44
fireworks	はなび	103
first-year student	いちねんせい	42
fishing	つり	147
five	ご (五)	44
flower arrangement	いけばな	105
flower viewing	はなみ	147
flute	フルート	62
food	たべもの	WB82
football	フットボール	59
foreign language	がいこくご	71
forty	よんじゅう (四十)	44
four	よん、し (四)	44
fourteen	じゅうよん、じゅうし	44
France	フランス	37
freelancer (writer, photographer)	じゆうぎょうしゃ	82
French (language)	フランスご	63
French (person)	フランスじん	37
Friday	きんようび (金よう日)	123
friend	ともだち	69
from (at the end of a letter)	…より	64
from … to …	…から …まで	132
from now	いまから	145
fun, enjoyable (*adj.*)	たのしい	133

G

garden	にわ	109
Geography (school subject)	ちり	71
German (language)	ドイツご	63
German (person)	ドイツじん	37
Germany	ドイツ	37
get up (out of bed) (*verb*)	おきます	137
glad, happy (*adj.*)	うれしい	116

Acknowledgements

The author expresses thanks to Toshiaki Kashihara, Leigh Kirwan, Sonoe Mifune and Yoshiyuki Setoguchi, who, throughout the writing of *Tsumiki*, answered numerous questions about the Japanese language.

She is also extremely grateful for the assistance provided by her editor Monica Pinda, who worked tirelessly and with good humour to complete this project.

She is particularly indebted to Yuka Ito, M.A. (Psycholinguistics), who provided on-line language assistance and grammatical explanations to ensure that the language introduced is correct, useful and authentic in Japan today.

The illustrations for the hiragana are adapted from *Hiragana in 48 Minutes*. Permission has been given by the publisher Curriculum Corporation, PO Box 177, Carlton South, Vic. 3053
http://www.curriculum.edu.au
Email: sales@curriculum.edu.au
Tel: (03) 9207 9600
Fax: (03) 9639 1616

The 46 mnemonic aids to the katakana script employed in *Tsumiki 1* have been reproduced from the Gold Coast Language Centre *Katakana Kit* developed by L. Kirwan. The author wishes to express her gratitude for permission to reuse these aids. Copies of the kit are available from:
L. Kirwan
Griffith University
Gold Coast Campus
Parklands Drive
Southport Qld 4215

Photographic credits

The author and publishers gratefully acknowledge the following for permission to reproduce photographic material: Australian Picture Library/Corbis/Bob Rowan, p 62 top right; Michael S Yamashita, p 62 bottom right; Bohemian Nomad Picture Makers, p 70 bottom right, p 148 bottom; William Dow, p 89 bottom left; photolibrary.com/Index Stock, p 62 bottom right, p 150 centre right; Jo Tayler, p 89 bottom right.

All other photographic material was supplied by the author.

Every effort has been made to trace and acknowledge copyright. If there has been any accidental infringement of copyright, the publishers apologise and would be pleased to obtain information to redress the situation.